# *Echoes From The Mills*

## *An Oral History*

## Also by Author

In Their Time (A Memoir)
Alone Together (Poetry)

# Echoes From The Mills

## An Oral History

*Franklin Mills, 1911*

Helen LaPlante Duchesne

by

Helen LaPlante Duchesne

For all the old memories

BEAR MOUNTAIN COVE PRESS
Publishers
Bristol • New Hampshire

Library of Congress Control Number: 2001130948

ISBN 0-9661940-1-2

Printed in the United States of America

*Dedicated to my father*

*J. Benjamin LaPlante*

*and*

*to the men and women*

*who appear in this book*

*and*

*to the men and women everywhere*

*who presently work or have worked*

*in the mills of America*

# Table of Contents

# Acknowledgements

I am deeply grateful to my sisters, Janet, Irene, Margaret, and Rita, and to my brother, Benjamin, for their helpful suggestions and encouragement while I was writing this book.

There were others: Maurice Hebert, who told me about his father and his five brothers working at the mill; Ronald Abear, a retired vice-president of operations at the L.W. Packard Mill in Ashland, New Hampshire, who helped me with the sequence of the cloth-making process; Albert Garneau, who answered some of my historical questions; Wayne Cilley, who toured the Stevens Mill building with me, and also told me about the comprehensive biography of the Stevens family; Paul Gagnon, curator of the Franklin Historical Society for making photographs available to me, and countless others who helped me to better understand the mill process.

Lastly, I am truly indebted to the people whose interviews appear in this book. Their willingness to share their mill years with me, as well as a part of their lives, is greatly appreciated. Without them, there would have been no story.

# Foreword

In September 1998, a four-alarm fire ravaged a section of the J.P. Stevens Company textile mill situated on the East Bow Street side of the Winnipesaukee River in Franklin, New Hampshire. The fire started in the water turbine area and moved upstream along the riverbank, as it burned the vacant, one long, continuous building. The intensity of the fire also damaged windows on the sixth floor of the main mill building, located across the river.

Stevens Mill was one of the last operating mills in Franklin. A typical, small New England mill town, Franklin is located in the heart of the Lakes Region. Facing a steadily declining market for its woolen goods and a growing flow of imported textiles, the mill closed its doors in 1970.

In its hey day, the mill had been one of Franklin's largest employers. Along with the nearby Stevens Mill in Tilton-Northfield, over 600 persons were employed at the two mills.

In 1999, as part of the $630,000 cleanup project after the fire, the nearby deteriorating 150 foot chimney was demolished. This landmark had towered over the mill complex and downtown business district for more than half a century.

There were numerous news stories in local and regional newspapers about these events. I read each article with sadness, as I remembered the people and events that had first made me aware of the mill and its workers. I was reminded of how my father and his family came from Canada to Franklin to work in the mills, first in Sulloway Hosiery Mill, and then in M.T. Stevens & Sons Mill, which later became J.P. Stevens Company.

My father worked in the mills long before I was born, but as we were growing up, he told us many stories about his days in the mills. And at one time or another, all of my paternal aunts and uncles worked at the mills, some of them for all of their working lives. I felt I had a connection to the mills, and the idea of working at the mills had always held a certain fascination and mystery for me.

Another contributing factor to my interest in the mills happened when I was young. My mother used to drive downtown with my brother, sisters and me to shop on a weekday afternoon between 2 and 4. We children waited in the car on Central Street in Franklin, usually in front of the First National Store or Raffaelly's Market or J.J. Newberry's, while she did her errands.

Smith Street was a short street between J.J. Newberry's and the First National Store, which led directly to Stevens Mill behind the business district. As we waited in the car, near this busy corner, we watched as large numbers of men and women came walking up or down Central Street, and turned into Smith Street on their way to the second shift in the mill. Many of the men held a cigarette in one hand and their black lunch boxes in the other. There was an enviable air of camaraderie among them. They seemed to be in step with one another, almost as if they were marching in a parade. I wondered what they were talking about, and oftentimes seeing them laughing, I wondered what could be so funny. I was curious about what was in their lunch boxes and if they felt as heavy as they looked.

Soon, another parade began as the first shift ended. This parade had a much slower pace as the weary men and women, carrying their empty lunch boxes and smoking their cigarettes, started the slow walk home. What did those men and women do there all day in the mill? What were they making? Did they enjoy each other's company as they worked? What was it like inside that big redbrick building?

Years later, when I read about the disastrous fire and the demolition of the giant chimney, I realized I wanted to know more about the mill and its people. I decided to interview former workers and to write their memories of the mill. I hoped I was not too late to learn their stories firsthand.

The land on which Stevens Mill sits was purchased in 1863. A group of businessmen, called The Franklin Falls Company, bought the 300–400 acres of property known then as the Elkins Land, and subsequently built the mill. The mill was situated along the south side of the Winnipesaukee River, a short distance north of Central Street, which is now Franklin's main business district. Griffin and Taylor Woolen Company was the first company to manufacture in the building, when they set up machinery for making woolens.*

---

**Information received from Albert Garneau, Franklin's local historian.*

The original Stevens Company was founded in 1813 in North Andover, Massachusetts, when Nathaniel Stevens and his partner, Dr. Joseph Kittredge, began to manufacture woolen goods. Nathaniel parted with Dr. Kittredge in 1831 and ran the business alone until his sons were old enough to become partners. In 1850, the company became Nathaniel Stevens & Sons. In 1870, Nathaniel Stevens & Sons Company bought the machinery of the Franklin Mills Company and began operations in Franklin. The firm consisted of Moses T. Stevens, George Stevens and Horace Stevens. After the death of George and Horace, Moses T. Stevens became sole proprietor of the business and, in 1876, changed the name of his firm to M.T. Stevens Company. In 1901, when his sons became old enough to join the business, the name of the firm was changed to M.T. Stevens & Sons. His son, Nathaniel Stevens, became president and Moses T. Stevens, Jr. served as clerk.*

In 1904, the nearby Aiken Mill, on the north side of the river and directly opposite Stevens Mill, was acquired and united by an enclosed bridge across the Winnipesaukee River, thus greatly increasing the size of the mill complex.

Still later, in 1948, the Stevens Company purchased Gibson's Woolen Mill off Park Street in Northfield, New Hampshire. While the building was physically located in Northfield on the east side of the Winnipesaukee River, it was generally referred to by most people as the Tilton mill. Surette Storage Battery occupied the building after the mill closed. This building also was destroyed by fire.

After World War II, when Moses' nephew, John P. Stevens, Jr. became president of Stevens Mill, the mill's name was changed from M.T. Stevens & Sons to J.P. Stevens Company.**

J.P.'s father had established a dry-goods commission house in New York City and had prospered by selling the products of his uncle's company.***

When J.P. Stevens Company celebrated its 150th anniversary in Franklin in 1963, there were sixteen regional offices located across the United States. Its fifty-five plants employed 35,000 workers, many of them in the South. The company's home office was in New York City.†

---

* *Nathaniel Stevens, 1786–1865,* An Account of His Life and The Business He Founded *by Horace Nathaniel Stevens,* 1946

** *Albert Garneau*

*** *Nathaniel Stevens,* 1786–1865

† The Franklin Journal Transcript, *July* 23, 1970

Beginning in January 1999 and continuing through the year 2000, I interviewed the people who appear in this book. I began with Albert Garneau who then suggested the names of several other people to contact. With each new interview, I learned of more people with whom to meet. There may have been other people who would have liked to be interviewed, but I either did not know who they were, or I could not reach them.

Generally, I asked specific questions of workers during the interviews such as: date of birth, shifts worked, years employed at the mill, job descriptions, likes and dislikes of working in the mill, comical incidents that happened while working, hobbies, membership in organizations, etc.

Nearly every former worker recounted good experiences. But there were a few who did not, and they were the ones who generally chose not to be interviewed. Some told me they did not want to relive the bad memories. One man who worked there for many years said he was not treated well and that the mill was a "hellhole."

I have placed the chapters in order of the years that people started working at the mill, beginning with the earliest, with one or two exceptions, where the interviewee's descriptions help to explain the mill process.

Except in the very simplest way, this book is not an attempt to explain the detailed manufacturing of cloth or the workings of the mill. Of that, much has already been written. Rather, it is for the people, who worked at Stevens Mill in Franklin, and in Tilton, to tell about their jobs, and to describe their impressions of the mill in their own words. I wanted to hear and record their stories.

Much like the strands of wool they spun, some of the stories overlap, with shared words and recollections that may be repetitive, but I wanted each person to have his say. I wanted to keep their memories alive.

In the telling of their stories I feel that these men and women have spoken for mill workers everywhere, those in the past and those working today. And because of their labors, our lives have been enriched.

As the editor, I have changed some phrases only for greater clarity and better readability. I trust I will be forgiven if I have not captured each person's exact words, meanings, or descriptions.



Helen L. Duchesne

# Prologue—
# Traveling in a Hayrack

In the late 1800s and early 1900s, most Canadian families were living on their own self-supporting farms. Farmers raised their own cattle, pigs and chickens, and used the meat, milk, eggs, and butter for themselves. They grew their own vegetables and had their own fruit trees.

Living on a farm was hard work. Children had many chores and were expected to help with the milking, care of the animals and haying, as well as planting, weeding, and harvesting the gardens.

Many people with large families found their farms too small to sustain the family. That is what happened to the Duval family who lived in Ste. Monique, Quebec, about seventy-five miles northeast of Montreal.

My paternal grandmother, Octavie Duval, was the fifth child in a family with nine children. She was thirteen years old in 1870, just five years after the United States Civil War. Her parents, Marie and Joseph Duval, realizing the farm was too small for their growing family, made the decision to go to the States to work in the textile mills. Their plan was to earn enough money to be able to return to Canada and buy a larger farm later on. Like most of the farm families who went to the States to work in the mills, with plans to return, the Duvals did not sell their farm. A relative or neighbor kept a careful watch over it while they were gone. Sometimes during the summer, a family member would return to visit friends and relatives, and to check on the farm.

Though the usual method of transportation to travel long distances was the train, for my great-grandparents and their large family, it was financially impossible. My father always told the story of how his mother and her family made the trip to Montpelier, Vermont in a hayrack with a pair of horses. (A hayrack is a wagon with a framework extending up and slightly out from the wagon to permit carrying large amounts of hay.)

The trip to the States probably took about a week. The hayrack carried only the family's essential belongings with some hay for the comfort of the mother and children. They brought their own food with them, packing ice in sawdust to keep the meat, milk, and butter cold. Some nights they may have found shelter in a friendly farmer's barn, while other nights they camped by the side of the road, sleeping in the hayrack, or on the ground wrapped in old quilts or a horsehair blanket. A campfire would have been a necessity to cook the evening meal, warm the family, and keep the wild animals away. The horses ate grass by the side of the road and drank water from brooks or streams, as well as at roadside watering troughs, common in those days. The family would learn of the many springs along the way from other travelers. (In fine weather all of this may have been an exciting journey, but I can't help wondering what it was like on a rainy day or during thunder showers while enroute.)

When the Duvals reached Montpelier, a relative or friend living there provided temporary housing. Most new arrivals went to towns or cities where relatives or friends already lived, getting their help with living arrangements and in obtaining a job.

After working in Montpelier for a while, the family moved to Claremont, New Hampshire, there again, to work in the mills. It is likely someone told them the pay was better there. The stay in Claremont was short-lived. Their desire to return to Canada to buy that dream farm was strong. Searching for even better pay, they were drawn to Manchester, New Hampshire, where many Canadians before them had gone in search of jobs.

Although just a young teen, my grandmother started work at the Amoskeag Mill. There, she learned to weave. "She was so short they had to make a little bench for her to stand on so she could reach over the shuttle to pass the thread through," my father said. Her earnings would have been given to her parents, for in that day, everyone was expected to contribute to the family's support.

After just a few years of working in the mills, the Duval family had saved enough money to return to Canada where they bought that large dreamed-of farm. My father always said, "They had a beautiful farm."

There are no stories to tell about what my grandmother did when she returned to Canada and to that new farm her parents had purchased. But I suspect she worked on it. After all, that was the reason for going to the States, to have a farm and enough land for the entire family.

However, four or five years later when Octavie was twenty-two years of age, she married my grandfather, Arestide LaPlante. They bought their own small farm with perhaps a dream of also going to the States. If so, it took a long time to happen. Over twenty years and thirteen children. Some dreams do take a long time!

# The LaPlante Family Goes to the States

My father, Joseph Benjamin LaPlante, was born in 1889, the seventh child of thirteen children born to my grandparents, Arestide and Octavie LaPlante. Their first two children died at birth and a third died in infancy. Of the ten surviving children, six were boys and four were girls.

My grandparents owned their own farm in Ste. Perpétue, Quebec, about seventy-five miles northeast of Montreal and approximately twenty-five miles southwest of Trois Rivières. It was a small farm and gradually, as the number of children increased, the farm could not produce enough to support the family. My grandparents decided to go to the States to work in the mills, as many other Canadian people had done. But unlike Octavie's family, not with the intent of eventually returning to Canada and purchasing a larger farm, but to settle in the States.

In 1903, when my father was fourteen years old, he and his family migrated to Franklin, New Hampshire. Arestide and Octavie, with their ten children, traveled by train from St. Perpétue to Montreal on the "Montreal" train, and from there to the Franklin Falls Railroad Station. The oldest child was twenty, the youngest, two years old.

Eugene LaPlante, a cousin, met them at the railroad station. "Eugene was the one who talked us into coming to Franklin," my father said. "There were ten children in his family too, and they had been living and working in Franklin for two or three years before we came. We came to Franklin because of them."

Eugene had arranged a tenement for the LaPlante family to rent at 53 Canal Street, just a "stone's throw away" from Stevens Mill. They lived on Canal Street until 1908 when my grandparents were able to buy their own home, and they moved to 75 School Street. My grandparents, an aunt, and several uncles continued to live there until the end of their lives. When the last family member, my Uncle Steve, died in 1969, the house was sold.

Upon the family's arrival at the train station, my father said they were met by men from Sulloway Mill who wanted Aristide to go to work right away. Since he spoke only French, my grandfather did not understand them. When an interpreter told him what they wanted, he replied, "Wait until I am settled!" He refused to go with them. But the next day he went to work at Sulloway Mill!

*Octavie LaPlante at 53 Canal Street, 1903 or 1904; left to right: Frank, Adelina, Octavie, Hector, Eva and Alvina.*

The mills badly needed people to work, my father said. "The Polish and Italians—all nationalities—came to Franklin just about the same time." Arestide worked in the pick room where wool was put in big machines to pull it apart and get it ready for carding. From there it was spun for the knitting machine. He worked from 6 A.M. to 6 P.M. and earned a dollar a day.

Ernest, who was the oldest boy at twenty, went to work right away, too. The others stayed home, helping with the household, while the four youngest children went to school.

My father had attended school in Canada until he was eleven. Now at fourteen, he was not required to go to school in the United States. After only two weeks, he too, went to work at Sulloway Mill, as did his brother, Stephen, and two of his sisters, Mary Louise and Adelina.

Mary Louise and Adelina worked in the winding room. "It had big bobbins wound with thread and the thread was used to knit with," my father said. Steve worked in the spinning room. Much like the farm they left in Canada, you might say working in the mill was a family affair.

My father thought children were allowed to begin working at the mills at the age of twelve. "Children were paid by how much work they did, or piecework, and not by the hour or day."

His first job was working with women who turned stockings. My father

*The author's father, Benjamin LaPlante, at left, Sulloway Mill, 1903 or 1904.*

described the job this way, "I had a big wagon (four wheels with a box on it) that was full of stockings. The women sat at a long table. I used to take a dozen stockings at a time and give them to this woman and that woman. They would put their hands in the stockings and check to make sure there were no holes in them."

Sometimes the stockings were put on an iron frame to be inspected. Workers were paid so much a dozen. "I think they paid a cent and a half, or was it two and a half cents a dozen?" my father said. "Anyway, it was awfully big pay!" Soon he, too, was promoted to turning stockings.

As a new immigrant, my father could not speak English, but by working with these women, it did not take him long to learn. According to my father, "Some of those women would say anything! One woman there especially—oh, she was a devil," he said laughing. "She came up behind me and said, 'Benne, you come over here. Go over to that woman and tell her....' Of course it was something bad. But I didn't know what she was talking about, because she said it in English. So I went and told the woman what she had said, and the first thing I knew I got slapped in the face. So when somebody else did the same thing, I went and had someone explain to me what it was and of course I didn't say that anymore!"

The Polish and the Italians learned English the same way, my father said.

"They learned to be careful of what they said too, because no one wanted a punch in the nose."

In spite of the work schedule, there was time to have fun. During the time my father turned stockings, he said, "There were six of us boys: Pete Bourque, Henry White, Nestor Deshaies and two others. The boss's name was Irving Davis—a big fellow. He used to come and sit on the edge of the table where we turned the stockings. One day Pete Bourque and Henry White took a great big safety pin and drilled a little hole in the table and tied a string underneath the table to the pin.

"Mr. Davis came by and sat on the table, because he used to come up and give us the devil if we didn't do the right thing. Some of those boys had been there a while and they liked to play tricks. So anyway, the boss came and sat down and was giving us the devil. Henry White was over there and he had the string down and he let it go. Mr. Davis jumped in the air and looked underneath, but couldn't find the darn thing. He said, 'Whoever did that is going to be fired!' Nobody said a word. We didn't know anything about it. We wanted to laugh, but we didn't dare to laugh, but it was so funny we did laugh!" my father said, chuckling at the memory.

After three or four months turning stockings, my father learned to knit. "You made so much a dozen for knitting too, but it was more pay than for turning stockings." He worked as a knitter at the mill for five or six years.

The tricks continued in the knitting room. "The same boss, Mr. Davis, would go around the machines telling us this and telling us that. We had two women who sat at the table turning tops. They had a ring with needles and they put the top of the stocking on it. We, the knitters, took that top and put it on the machine to start the stocking. When the boss came around, someone would take a stocking and hitch it with a safety pin to the back of his jacket and everyone would laugh. They played tricks all the time. It was fun and we learned English pretty fast.

"Sometimes there were women in the seaming room where you walked in an alley between two tables. Some women would come up, and it was a dirty thing to do, and they'd slip your pants down! The boss caught two or three of them and fired them. In the mills there were tricks, but, as I said, you learned fast in those days!"

When Sulloway Mill started to slow down, my father went to work at Stevens Mill. He began by folding cloth on the folding machine. Then he learned to weave. "That was better money," he said.

In 1911, he left the mill for a summer job as a caretaker at the Aiken Manor on Webster Lake. During the wintertime, he would get a job wherever he could, usually doing mill work. Then in 1917, he began working for the Aikens year round. Still later, he became a farmer caretaker at the Marcy Farm, also on Webster Lake, where he remained for the rest of his working days. He worked until he was eighty years old. He used to tell us he preferred working in the outdoors where he could enjoy nature rather than being closed inside a mill all day.

My father particularly liked to tell the story about his trying to enlist in the army during World War I. Many of the men he knew were leaving the mills and going into the service. He thought it would be exciting to see the world and so he tried to join, too. But he was turned down because he had false teeth. "I told the brass, 'I'm not going over to bite the enemy; I'm going over to fight the enemy!" he said. Later, he was allowed to replace someone who could not serve. He had just boarded a ship to go oversees when the armistice was signed. He never did fulfill his dream of seeing the world.

Every Sunday during my childhood after attending church, we visited my grandmother, Octavie, and the aunts and uncles on School Street. My grandfather had died when I was a little girl. He had worked in the mill until he died. My grandmother could not speak English and we children could not speak French. A fun-loving family, the relatives liked to tell stories and jokes, many of them about their work and co-workers in the mill. Usually the stories were told in both French and English—at the same time! Someone would begin a story in English and when it was time for the punch line, they would switch to French and everyone would laugh and laugh. I suspect the punch line was not for children's ears, but it was frustrating not to know the ending of the story.

Although I was glad not have an accent myself, I loved listening to my father's French accent. He was a small wiry man and it seemed to fit his easygoing personality. Many people knew him and everyone loved him. He lived almost ninety-seven years. As Virginia Dufault, an interviewee in this book, once said, "It seemed like he lived forever." I wish he had!

# Albert Garneau

*Albert Garneau, Christmas 1992*

I arrived at Albert's house on a cold, January day following several bad ice storms. Everyone's yard was a sheet of ice for weeks and his was no exception.

Albert proudly told me he is of French descent. He was born on February 2, 1919 in St. Johnsbury, Vermont. When he was four years old, his family moved to Franklin, New Hampshire, where he has remained all of his life. He and his wife, Eugenia, have a son and a daughter.

Albert did not pass the physical examination required to get into the service during World War II, because he had a heart murmur. He said he did not really want to go, but he felt bad about it, because a lot of other men were going, and he thought he should serve, too. Referring to his heart, he added, "And here I am still alive and some of them are dead!"

Albert explained that while many French people came to the States from Quebec to work in the mills, his father's cousin came specifically to learn English. At only eighteen, his cousin figured out the easiest way to learn the language was to move to the States for a couple of years. Albert said, "He learned English right out of Stevens Mill. Later, after returning to Quebec, he became head of the Provincial Police, a big wheel."

Albert worked at Stevens Mill in Franklin during two different stretches, for six or seven months at a time, first in 1938, and again in 1942. He said he had been working here and there doing lots of different jobs, like digging ditches and working on roads, but business was terrible. So, at eighteen, he tried to get into Stevens Mill.

He knew William Edwards, who was a boss at the mill. He also knew that

Mr. Edwards walked every morning from his home on Prospect Street down to the mill. Albert decided he would stand on Smith Street, the street to the mill, where Mr. Edwards would not see him until he turned the corner.

"Then I'm facing him. I'm right there! So this day he comes around the corner and I say, 'Good morning, Mr. Edwards. I'm looking for a job.'" Mr. Edwards told Albert that he did not think he knew how bad business really was. How the mill was trying to keep its help, those who had been there for years, and especially those with families. Albert replied that he had a pretty good idea.

The next morning Albert was right there in the same place and met Mr. Edwards again. Mr. Edwards said, "I thought I told you yesterday. . . !" Albert continued, "To cut a long story short, I went eight days in a row, and on the eighth day when I came around the corner, Mr. Edwards asked me if I knew Frank Stott, the boss in the dry finish room and how to get there. He told me to tell Mr. Stott that Mr. Edwards had hired me and to put me to work.

"That's how I got in at Stevens Mill. That's a good story, isn't it?" I had told Albert I was looking for good stories. I had to agree his story was a very good story. He added, "When I was looking for a job, I knew better than to bring two or three guys with me, because your chances are about a million to one of getting one." He pointed to his head and said, "I had a little bit up here."

On that eighth morning when Albert got to the mill, he went directly to Frank Stott and told him what Mr. Edwards had said. Mr. Stott never questioned it. He took Albert to Joe Cleary to work in dry finish, but before long Albert was put in styling.

The styler was the last person to touch the cloth before it was papered for shipping. The bolt came with a tag in it. Albert had to remove the tag, weigh the bolt, record the color, batch number, and lot number. When he finished, he replaced the tag, and put the bolt on one of the big tables lined up by the windows. The cloth could not be papered until Mr. Edwards came in and initialed it.

Albert said a man named Hayes put the paper on the bolts, but if Albert knew how the paper was put on he did not tell me. He got sidetracked with a story, and after all, I was looking for stories!

Albert recounted, "Hayes had put an ad in the newspaper to a lonely hearts club. He had these damn letters from all over the country. He had pictures of all these women and they wanted to marry him. I never forgot that! It's embedded in my mind."

Another man who worked at the mill was Billy Harper. Billy was the shear machine operator. The shear cut a piece of cloth to a certain thickness. Albert said he never ran a shear, but he thought the cloth was napped and sheared at the same time. "You know, it was a long time ago—over sixty years! Anyway, it was a big machine and the cloth had to feed through it. A large basket was under it.

"When Billy finished his shift, he went to Dan Cote's lunchroom, bought some clams and a six-pack, and returned to the mill. There he ate his supper. Then he'd go to sleep in the basket under the shear. He did that night after night. Mr. Edwards would come in and check that shear—stand right there, feeling that cloth—and looking it over! His foot was probably only two feet away from Billy's head as he slept in that basket of the shear. Mr. Edwards never caught him, or he knew he was there and just let him stay. I never forgot that either!"

Laughing, Albert told me the men in the mill had different signals to let each other know when a boss or one of the inspectors was coming. At the first sight of one of these men approaching a downstairs room, someone would rap on the pipe and stand at the bottom of the stairs. That was a clue for someone in the upstairs room to appear at the top of the stairs. If Bill Edwards was coming, the signer moved his hand across the top of his body. If it was Fred Durham, the assistant superintendent, the signer moved his hand across the middle part of his body, and if it was Frank Stott, the movement was across the lower part of his body.

One thing Albert wanted me to understand was that many of the men played a lot of poker. They received their pay in cash Friday evening as they worked. "We got paid Friday night and these guys would start right in playing poker. They don't wait until twelve o'clock. Understand now, they're playing poker on Stevens' time."

I naively asked, "For money?" And he said, "Of course for money!" Then in a loud convincing voice he went on to say he never played on company time! "I was the guy they probably should have tied the wings to, because I figured anybody who's paying me—that's one principle I had - anyone who was paying me was entitled to get something for their money.

"And I loved to play poker! I played poker in every damn block in town until the sun was rising, and I never should have done that either. I played poker when I was earning sixteen bucks a week—fifty cents to a buck on a card—and I shot pool with the best of them."

The second time Albert was hired, he began in wet finish on the same day as Cy Wescott with Pete Sharlotte as the boss. They ran the nappers. Albert also worked on the carbonizer. He said it was a big long machine—maybe fifty feet long. The cloth ran through a tank with chemicals in the water. "And all you did was sit there and watch and make sure the cloth didn't, I don't know, didn't get out of line or screw the machine up or what—you know, it was a long time ago! Eventually, the cloth folded out into a hand truck. Harold Bennett worked on the end of the folder while I worked in the middle." I told Albert he worked so long ago I did not see how he could remember as much as he did. But he said he could see everything right there in his mind.

He wanted to be sure to tell me about the tanks in the dye house which he also called kettles. Irving Beaupre and Edgar Menard worked there. Albert said it was not a bad job. He did not know if they were supposed to or not, but on Friday nights the men would go over there, put the right temperature water in the huge, stainless steel kettles, and take a bath. "Damn good place to take a bath!" Albert said.

After two and one half hours, Albert still had a story to tell. "Some things impress you working at the mill and you never forget it. There was a guy named Blake. He had an oil can that held maybe a gallon or two of oil with a gol' darn spout probably eight feet high and he'd walk around the mill looking for shafts. I never forgot that! I can still see that guy oiling those shafts with that thing ten feet over his head." And I think Albert could, because he related the whole story while looking up at the ceiling.

As I listened to Albert talk and reminisce about the years he worked at Stevens Mill, I learned much of Albert's life as well. He is a delightful storyteller with a head full of historical information. He obviously has been a very busy man over the years with his wood business, photography, civic services, and love of history. He is also quite a philosopher, as I have found many to be who have experienced life over "the long haul." He told me he frequently writes articles for the Franklin newspaper, *The Telegram*, and has for many years. He also enjoys clipping newspaper articles and collects them in his many files.

At the end of our interview I asked Albert if he thought people enjoyed working in the mill and he said, "Oh yes, it was their life. It was an education!"

Albert told me how he had learned to take it slow with his wood business and bide his time. "You have to keep working at it and someday the pie changes. And then people say, 'You know, that Garneau ain't a bad guy.'" I had to agree!

# Freddye Whiting

It was World War II and America was at war. Freddye began at Stevens Franklin Mill in 1941 as a clerk, but six months later her work at the mill was for the United States government.

"I did all the hand printing and finger printing, and all the histories that had to go to the FBI," Freddye said. "In fact I worked with an FBI agent and didn't even know it!"

Because the mill was making blankets for the United States Army, security concerns were high. "The government and the owners of the mill had to be very careful about everyone who worked there. They wanted to know how long each worker had worked, where they had come from, and what their backgrounds were. There were three to four hundred workers and even those who had been there for a long time had to go through the screening process. They also had to have an ID number." There were people of German ancestry, and Freddye knows now it was wrong, but it was believed that some people had to be watched. As it turned out, however, everyone proved to be trustworthy.

Freddye was born in Franklin on May 17, 1922, and except for a brief time when she was first married, she has lived in Franklin all of her life. She continues to live in the house that her husband built. She said proudly, "All by himself."

She was just nineteen in 1941 when she began working at the mill, after attending Concord Business College for one year. She worked for eighteen months until she got married. As a clerk, she said, "I took time cards from all the different departments to the girl who did the payroll. I also did odd jobs—letters when the secretary didn't have time—hit or miss—a little bit of everything."

Freddye laughed about how she got the job. At the time, her dad was the assistant superintendent of the plant. She said, "He was one of those dyed in the wool, do it right kind of men!" When she finished her first year of business school she did not want to return the second year. She was engaged to be married by then and decided she would just get a job.

One day she met Mr. Edwards, the superintendent of the mill, on the street going to work. She described him as "...a funny, old guy, kind of heavy, and he kind of teetered when he walked, always had a cigar stuck in his mouth. He was a character!"

Freddye said they were in front of Raffaelly's Market when the Raffaelly's daughter, Lena, was coming out. Mr. Edwards gruffly asked Lena, in a kidding way, what she was doing out of work at the mill, to which she responded that she was not off work, it was her time off! She looked at Freddye and asked what she was doing, and if she was going back to school. When Freddye told her she was not, Lena asked if she wanted her job, because she was getting married. Freddye looked at Mr. Edwards who told her to come in and apply. She said, "But Dad wouldn't allow it!" However, she did apply and got the job. When she went to work the following Monday, she said, "Dad nearly passed out!"

I was excited to learn that Freddye knew Nathaniel Stevens, a namesake for his grandfather, who was president of the company during the time that she was there. She said everyone called him Nat. "He had mills all over the New England states. I think the Franklin mill was one of his particular likes. He came from North Andover, Massachusetts, and made a point of coming up to visit—often!" She thought perhaps it was because Mr. Edwards was a good friend of his. "A stooped, older man with a shuffle, Mr. Stevens arrived in a limousine driven by a chauffeur. We'd see him coming from the office window and say, 'Oh boy, here comes Nat.' He knew everybody by their first names. He'd come into the office and say, 'How are you girls?' Big, tall, friendly man!"

Mr. Stevens remembered Freddye's dad, Fred Durham, from the time he started as a handyman, while he was still a high school student. After attending business college, Fred went back to Stevens as a clerk for a couple of years before serving in World War I.

Since he had been a superintendent at the mill, I asked Freddye to tell me a little more about her dad. She said Stevens Mill had told him he could have his job back when he was discharged from the army, so after serving for four or five years, he returned to the mill.

Fred lost a lung in the war and was sent to a hospital in Atlanta. While there he met Freddye's mother, Dessel. She was from Alabama and met Fred when she was visiting a patient in the bed next to his. They married and decided to make Franklin their home.

"Working at the mill was his life," Freddye added. "He started at the bottom and he went to the top. A local boy, Dad was a man who put everything he had into his job. He loved the mill; he loved the people, and they loved him."

Freddye described the layout of the building that she worked in, as it was when she there. "The office was on the front of the building and had a large window which looked out over the parking lot. That part of the building has since been taken down and does not even look the same.

"To the right of the office, a hallway led to stairs that went to the second floor. It was a large area where all the looms for spinning and weaving were located. The finishing department was upstairs, too. Steps and stairs went to a basement under the office. A tunnel led to the dye house—a long, low-slung building to the right of the office—where Mr. Innis had his vats. The building had large vents in the ceiling and you could smell the dyes outside. On the other side of the office was the remnant shop where the ends of bolts of cloth from the mill were sold, both to the public and to mill workers. The burling and carding rooms, as well as shipping and receiving, were in the back of the building. Vern Shaw was in charge of the shipping and receiving department." Freddye recalled the huge, old Mac truck—"the worst looking old thing you ever saw"—that brought the bags of raw material from the railroad station to the receiving room.

She enjoyed her work at the mill. "It was different every day. You never had the same thing over and over and I like variety. I enjoyed every minute."

Another thing that Freddye enjoyed in the mill was meeting people of different nationalities: Polish, Italians, Greek, Albanians and French. "It was a real melting pot," she said.

Freddye stated, "No one fooled around very much because it was war time, and everyone was kind of on the sober side. We had lost people from the mill going into the service, and then we didn't know what to expect. It was not the gayest time in the world, at least it seemed that way to me."

Stevens had a bell tower with a bell that rang at 7 A.M., 12 P.M., and 4 P.M. Freddye said, "Bell ringing in town was important to many people. It announced when it was time to go to work, when business was to start, as well as marking the time to go to school."*

---

* *The bell was cast at the McShane Bell Foundry in Baltimore, Maryland, in 1887. When the mill closed in 1970, the bell was removed from the tower and sent to the company's headquarters in North Andover, Massachusetts.*

*Roger Smith with Nerie Poirier, Stevens Mill bellringer, undated.*

From the beginning of our interview, Freddye wanted to be sure to tell me about the mill bell ringer, Nerie Poirier. An elderly man, he rang the bell at the mill for many years. "He was so faithful with that bell ringing. He was quite a man and everybody knew him by his first name. Bless his heart, he did little odd jobs, emptied waste paper baskets, and pushed a mop around."*

Freddye and her husband, Eugene, had one daughter. Now a widow, Freddye keeps busy with birding and gardening, two hobbies that she really enjoys. She belongs to the Audubon Society and used to travel on many of their trips. Beautiful carved birds made by her husband are displayed in her kitchen. She says he was a good carpenter! "The garden keeps me busy all summer," she said, as she showed me colorful photos of her flower garden taken in the back yard.

---

* *In a note from Rachel Mercier, I learned that Nerie was born in Canada in 1870. He died in 1964 at ninety-four years of age. His family came to the States in 1896. They bought one of the mill-owned houses on Prospect Street. He began working at M.T. Stevens in 1897, retiring in 1953, when he was eighty-four years old. He worked for the company for fifty-six years.*

# Herbert Shaw

I met Herbert on a warm, cloudy day in December at his Tilton home, nestled among the pine trees. Dressed in a light sweater, he told me about the wild turkeys he feeds that come to his yard. He said they like the shelter of the tall trees.

Herbert was born in Salisbury, New Hampshire on June 12, 1914. He grew up there on a farm in a large family. He began working at the Stevens Franklin Mill at age twenty-three, in the fall of 1937. Shortly thereafter, he married his wife, Lou, (now deceased). They had one son. He worked at the Franklin mill for seventeen years and then at the Tilton mill for another seventeen years.

Herbert worked the first shift all of the years that he was employed at the mill. He said he was very lucky to be able to do that. Generally people worked their way from third shift to second and then to days. He started working when Bill Edwards was superintendent of the mill. Other superintendents he mentioned were: Richard Clarenbach, Roger Smith, Robert Dinan, Fred Durham, and James Horman.

In describing his first job at the mill, Herbert said he worked in the pick room. "The pick room gets the wool ready for the card room. There would be maybe a dozen different kinds of wool in one lot that the picker blended to make cloth. A little bit of oil was put on it, so the wool wouldn't fly around." I asked if he thought the wool flying around and getting into people's lungs was dangerous. He said it probably was, but he did not think it had bothered him and at the time he never thought about it.

"From the pick room, the wool went to the card room, then to the spinning room and finally to the weave room," he said. When the cloth was finished in the weave room, it was sent to dyeing and finishing. Herbert also worked in the card room for a number of years, as a finishing attendant for Tony Partelo. He said you could see fibers flying around the card room, too. "It looked like dust flying around." He found sitting and doing the same thing in the card room to be rather boring. Later on he worked in the shipping and receiving department.

When Herbert went to the Tilton mill, he worked in maintenance. He said there were lots of different things to do there. He worked on machinery, as well as putting on clapboards and sanding floors. "We had some hardwood floors and they looked beautiful." He and his partner also helped load and unload material from trucks. Of the many jobs he held at the mill, Herbert preferred maintenance, because he was doing different jobs every day of the week.

"I liked working in the mill. I had lots of nice friends," he said. "Stevens was a good place to work! I had no problems. I really liked all the superintendents and they were easy to work for. Some of them wondered why I was working there and told me I could make much more money somewhere else. But I didn't care, because what counts is whether you're satisfied and enjoying what you are doing. They didn't pay big money but I always got along great."

Hebert told me a story that he said was funny for him, but not for the man he worked with. "There was a pipe line that went from the downstairs drinking fountain into a big outlet pipe, and then into the river. Bill Sullivan in the weave room and some of the other guys used to chew snuff. When they got a drink of water at the fountain, they would wash their mouths out and spit in the drain, which plugged up the pipe.

"The thing was running over one day. They called us up to see if we could do something with the pipe. I got an air hose downstairs and plugged it into the other end of the big pipe. I told my partner to go upstairs and tell me when it was cleaned out, but to put a cloth over the pipe first, so the stuff wouldn't fly into his face. Well, he didn't get it on in time and all the brown stuff came up in his face and he was not very happy!"

Another incident he spoke of happened after an ice storm. The parking lot was filled with ice and looked like an ice pond. Some of the men carried their skates with them in their cars and when they got to work, they put them on and skated into the building. Herbert wondered if any of us would think to do something like that today.

When I questioned Herbert whether there was anything he didn't like about working in the mill, there was a long silence. Finally he said, "It's strange, I just can't think of anything. If it had been bad, I would have gotten out. No, I can't think of anything. Sure in the winter time it was cold taking wool from one side of the river across the bridge to the other side, but you had clothes on. It was just like chopping wood. If you're out chopping wood you can't blame anybody if it's cold, it's just part of living."

He continued, "Sometimes in Tilton we had to chop ice off the roof when it was below zero. That was a miserable job, but it was part of the job. We didn't complain about it. We just did it!"

While working at the mill was his main occupation, Herbert was also an antique collector. It began as a hobby. He said he was always busy buying and fixing up things he bought, and then selling them. He and his wife also owned property at Hampton Beach, where they spent time before and after the season, and rented to guests during the summer.

After he finished working in the mill, he worked with his antiques full time. With some surprise he said, "I ended up making more money than I did working in the mill." Some people had told him he should have done that a long time ago, but he wanted to make sure he had a regular pay check to pay his bills. That regular pay check was important to everyone I talked with!

As for organizations, Herbert said he was not a joiner. He and his wife always had a good time and a good life together and he did not need other things, especially with his antiques. He has a workshop in his house and he still repairs and finishes furniture.

Herbert was spontaneous and gracious. His infectious smile and the importance to him of being a part of the mill's history made talking with him a pleasure.

# William Fisher*

*William B. Fisher at his desk in J.P. Stevens, 1969*

My interview with Bill Fisher took place at the Merrimack County Nursing Home in Boscawen. His social worker had been in touch with him about my interviewing him, and he was pleased to talk with me. He was worried that he would not be very helpful, because he said his memory was not very good. I assured him that anything he had to offer was worthwhile.

Bill was born in Manchester on July 6, 1906. He attended Manchester schools and was a graduate of the University of New Hampshire. He moved to Franklin in 1950 to accept a position in the office of Stevens Mill, and worked there until the mill closed in 1970. "I interviewed the people that we hired," he said. I asked if he also fired people and he said that was not his job.

Although he could not remember, other former employees told me that he was the manager of the main office. They reported that he was very well liked because of his kindness, understanding, and humor.

I asked Bill if he had any interesting stories and he said, "I have to give that a thought, but I probably have. It'll take me a while to bring it to the surface." I told him I would give him a minute to bring it to the surface,

---

* *Died July 23, 2001*

and he replied that he guessed he would need more than a minute!

Bill's answer was a quick "Yes" when I asked him if he enjoyed working in the mill. He said, "They were reliable, honest people to work with and for." I told Bill what an affirmation and wonderful statement his one sentence conveyed about the company that so many people worked for. He later said the company was very conscious of its employees' welfare, a "good place to work."

Playing poker was one of Bill's hobbies. Again, I foolishly asked, "For money?" I guess we all know the answer.

His wife died several years ago. Being a family man with two sons, Bill said that working around the house had kept him busy. He remembered painting his house and told me he had good neighbors.

At the time of his death, I learned Bill had been a member of the New Hampshire House of Representatives and the Franklin City Council. He also belonged to The Franklin Historical Society, New Hampshire Historical Society, New Hampshire Audubon Society, and the Veterans of Foreign Wars.

# Roger (Huck) Hebert

Roger told me everyone calls him Huck and that most people do not even know his real first name. He explained that he got the name Huck when the Regal Theater in Franklin was running a contest during a showing of Huckleberry Finn. Anyone dressed as Huckleberry Finn could get into the show free. "So," Roger said, "I had the big straw hat and the big holey overalls and I had three of my friends with me." When the boys started to go in with all of Roger's "stuff," the man who collected the tickets put up both hands and said, "Whoa, hey, wait a minute, where're you all going?" His friends said, "We're his managers; we dress him." So all four were allowed into the theater. Only three moviegoers were dressed as Huckleberry Finn, and Roger won the contest. "Ever since," he said, "Huck was on all my school papers and it followed me right into the service." Even today, Roger said most people say, "Hi Huck."

Immediately, I had a hint that Huck had a good sense of humor and could tell a good story. I told him I was looking for good stories. I was not disappointed.

Huck was born on April 26, 1925. He and his wife, Jenny, have a son and a daughter. He started working at the Franklin mill in 1946, at age twenty-one, after a three year stint in the navy. He continued until the mill closed.

Huck recounted that at one time J.P. Stevens in Franklin was a complete woolen mill. This meant the whole cloth-making process, beginning with the raw wool to the finished material (ready for sale) was done there. After the company purchased Gibson's Woolen Mill in Tilton, all manufacturing was done in Tilton, and Franklin became just a finishing and dyeing mill.

As a finishing and dyeing mill, cloth also came from other Stevens' mills to be finished, such as those in Merrimack, New Hampshire and North Andover, Massachusetts. "When those mills sent their cloth to Franklin, they were like a customer," Huck said. "We had to keep track of all the yardage they sent up."

During his years at the mill Huck held many jobs. He worked second shift in dry finish, first shift in wet finish and later in dry finish perching (inspecting). He also was a sample expediter. A sample expediter facilitated and oversaw the speed or action of the cloth, as it progressed through the mill for quick delivery to the customer.

Huck gave me a rather comprehensive description of the processes that the cloth went through. "First part, naturally, you had to get the wool." He laughed and laughed, and I laughed too. I agreed and said, "Naturally." Staple wool and the highest priced wool for worsted were delivered in huge bales wrapped in burlap. The wool was dumped into the picker house where the picker machine tore the wool apart. Oil dumped into the machine helped to blend the wool fibers together and kept the pieces from flying about.

After the picker process, the wool went to the card room where five or six large machines made the wool into an untwisted rope. From there, it went to spinning and then to weaving. After the weaving process it was inspected, a job done by women called burling. Tweezers were used in this process to take imperfections out of the cloth.

Following the examination of the cloth, it was taken to the carbonizer. The carbonizer was a huge machine, probably thirty feet long according to Huck. When it was purchased, a new section had to be built onto the mill. The cloth first went into a tank of water, then it was transferred to a tank of sulfuric acid. The sulfuric acid burned all the ingredients out of the cloth except the wool.

From there, the cloth went to yet another water bath and then into a dryer. The dryer was called a baker because of the high heat it reached. Pins on each side of the machine carried the cloth along.

Talking about the carbonizer reminded Huck of a story. He said the mill shut down on Saturday nights at midnight and reopened at midnight on Sundays. When the amount of cloth that was folded out into trucks from the carbonizer got low, another piece had to be sewn on. The Sunday night person would start the machine, and it usually took about twenty minutes for the cloth to come out the other end. A big mirror at the end of the machine allowed the operator to see where the folder went back and forth, folding the cloth out into the truck. "Well, on this particular night," Huck said, "the guy started that machine going and he looked in the mirror, but it only showed the side of the folder. Twenty minutes went by and the folder was still going, yet he couldn't see any edges of cloth. After about thirty-five minutes, I called out, 'What's happening?' The guy went to check and found the folder was still going, but the cloth inside the baker had slipped off the pins so it was going out through the exhaust and onto the front lawn! It took several men to clean it all up and when the boss found out about it the operator was fired!

"After the carbonizing and the baker process, the next step was going to the pounders. As the cloth ran through the machine, big wheels came down and pounded all the black imperfections out of the cloth. From there, it went to the fulling mills, which shrank the cloth; otherwise, it looked like loosely woven burlap."

When Huck worked in the wet finish department, he became a wet steamer operator. "A wet steamer puts a shine on the cloth. They had a water finish and a steam finish. A steam finish was much more expensive. If you put the cloth side by side you couldn't tell the difference, but once you sent the water-finished cloth to the dry cleaners, it would lose all of its luster. The steam finish maintained the luster no matter how many times you sent it to the cleaners."

The steamers were located on one side of the dye house. "The cloth was on a cylinder and steamed three rolls at a time. The cylinder was probably a foot and a half in diameter and had a lot of holes in it. The cloth had to be wet first and then the steam came in on both sides, so it could penetrate up through the cloth. Next, the valves were opened to let the steam out. Finally, cold water was placed in the kettle. Now if you opened up the valves too fast, the cloth—three or four layers of it next to the roll—would shift. It would look like an accordion. That was bad and had to be thrown away." I asked if they were watched by their bosses to make sure that did not happen and Roger responded, "Oh yeah!"

Roger also ran the brushes that brushed the nap so that it would go in one direction. Different finishes called for different machines, such as grazing the nap on the cloth. From there the cloth went to the dye house for dyeing.

There were stainless steel kettles in the dye house, as well as wooden kettles. So much cloth was running through the wooden kettles that often wooden fibers got mixed in. "When Stevens bought their biggest stainless steel kettle, they practically had to take out one side of the dye house to get the kettle in the room," Huck said.

Some of the cloth went to the dryer for the dry finish process. The cloth was pulled up on a roller through a slit in the floor, as it went through a series of folders into trucks. Once the trucks got full, the workers tore the cloth and put another truck under the machine.

After filling so many trucks, depending on how it was processed, the cloth was sent to the shear. "There were about five or six shears, large machines that had razor sharp, spiral things on two rolls, one above and one in the middle," Huck said. "The cloth was threaded into the machine and the machine sheared all that nap off. You had to make darn sure you kept your eye open because there were two levers, one for the upper cutter, and one for the lower cutter, and if the seam got cut, you had to shut down the machine and rethread."

Fancy worsted and gabardines could not be sheared close enough, so they were singed using a new machine called a singer, which ran by gas. The singer had a pipe with holes in it that went the width of the machine. When lit, flames came out of the holes, as the cloth went underneath it. At one time, Huck said they had an assistant finisher who came to the mill, and the regular finisher was "kind of skeptical of him."

At this point Huck was already laughing. "The cloth going through was a fancy worsted, blended with nylon. So, not realizing, the assistant finisher ran the cloth through the singer. When it got to the other end, the singer had burned out all the nylon, so the cloth looked like a screen!

"Depending on the desired finish, some of the cloth had to be pressed. It went to a machine called the semi-decater which gave it a soft finish. The cloth went on a steel cylinder with brass jackets that closed around the cloth as it passed through the cylinders. The cloth was pressed when the steam was turned on."

From time to time, Huck had to stop and think of the next process as if placing himself back at the mill fifty years ago. He continued, "From there, the cloth went to the perch line to be examined. It came over rolls in front of big picture windows in the back of the room so imperfections could be seen. Any imperfections required a string in the edge of the cloth. When finished and rolled up to ship to the customer, the strings were counted. For each string that was in the piece, the customer was allowed an eighth of a yard that they didn't have to pay for, called 'dead loss.'"

Huck went on to explain the term, dead loss. "Much of the nap was lost from the cloth after all the operations it went through. The finisher determined how full the cloth should be to have it come out according to customer specifications when it was finished. Each style of cloth had a sheet that came from the designers at the weaving mill with the whole history of the cloth: shrinkage, dead loss, width, finish width, loom width, etc.

"After examining the cloth, it went to the winder. The fella had to keep his eye out to watch the edge of the cloth for how many strings it had, and if it had white tape that would mean a cutout (a bad piece) or remnant. After the cloth was rolled up and the strings and tape were in there, the bolt of cloth was put on a conveyor belt and weighed. If something started at 1,000 pounds and ended up at 800, then 200 pounds was dead loss."

After all the handling and processing the cloth had undergone, it had to be washed. From the washer, it was dried and then sent to the top floor where the final perching or examining was done. Huck said if there were bad imperfections, menders would have to be called. Menders were women who weaved by hand and repaired the damaged parts.

When Huck finished telling me about the different operations of the mill, he said, "I went through practically the whole mill except the grey room, but I was down there constantly. It was called the grey room because the cloth was unfinished, not yet dyed, and had a greyish color. When I was an expediter, I went down there to see if orders had been received in from the weaving mill. Every kind of cloth that came into the mill—they called them cuts—came into the grey room with a weaving ticket."

Huck went on to tell me there were different areas where the men ate lunch, "little cubicles really," to eat and to smoke, because they could not smoke on the machines. "Some smoked more than others, but they were allowed three smokes a day at five minutes each smoke." I said, "For those addicted that must have been hard." But Huck said people sneaked out the back door for smokes. He laughed when I commented, "And some people still do."

I asked if the workers played tricks, told jokes and talked a lot on the job. He said not really because the second hand bosses (the foremen) were continually walking up and down to make sure everyone was working! Even though Huck had answered "Not really" to my question, he was ready to tell me more stories now that his description of the making of cloth was finished.

"The mill used to shut down for lunch at twelve noon and reopen at one o'clock. There was a long bench in the tunnel where men changed from their street clothes into old shoes or boots and into overalls or old clothes to work in the mill. There was one man who never started to get ready to go to dinner until two minutes before twelve. Then he had to rush like hide to change his clothes and put his shoes on. Shoes were put on a big wooden plank on the floor. Well, this day the guys thought they would have a good time with this guy who was always late. So they stapled this fella's shoes to the plank. He slipped both feet into his shoes and then started to slide but they wouldn't move! Then everybody started laughing.

"There was this other person who worked second shift, 3 P.M. to 11 P.M., in the wet finish department and he was afraid of his own shadow. This man was awful nervous. So to have a good time with him they built a big cross on wood and covered that cross with a big, thick, white sheet. Across the river, just a little below the mill, The Public Service Company had a footbridge that went to Bow Street. Some fellas went to the end of the bridge and screwed in a big pulley and then ran a rope over the top of that white sheet through the pulley, and pulled it over to the window. So when this guy went by, they'd pull and it would come up like a ghost. Well, that guy from that point on, didn't turn his back to the window the rest of the night, and he didn't come to work the next day. His boss found out about it—and was he mad! He said if he ever caught the guy that did that he'd fire him."

Another story Huck had heard, but had not actually seen himself, concerned two women who stole some worsted cloth. They sent it to Worcester, Massachusetts, and had slacks made out of the material. "Then, one day they were foolish enough to wear them to work!" Huck said. All of a sudden, the superintendent happened to see the material and he recognized it. He said, "Where did you get those slacks?" The women told him they had bought them someplace and he said, "That's funny, that style hasn't even been released yet!"

Huck also enjoyed telling me about the young man who came up to him after lunch one day and said, "You know I'm selling cars now and I see you're about ready to swap."

"Yes, I am."

"What kind would you like?"
"I'd like a Dodge Monaco."
"What color?"
"I'd like to have a green one."
"Do you want automatic shift?"
"Oh yeah."
"What size wheels do you want?"
"Fifteen inch would be all right."
"When do you want delivery of that?"
"Any time. But the only thing is, who's going to pay for that?"
And of course Huck laughed and laughed.

He seemed proud of the fact that J.P. Stevens sponsored a family day event every year, sometimes at Bear Brook State Park, or at Gunstock Recreation Area. Lots of different activities were planned.

One activity for the young children was for them to find 500 pennies in a big pile of sawdust. Whoever found the most pennies received a prize. "The only problem with that game was that the parents were in the sawdust trying to find the pennies too, so the prize really went to the parents!" he said.

One time a little girl came up to Huck all excited and said, "Look at the ribbon I won for third prize." He asked her how many children were in the contest and she said, "Three." Huck really laughed at that one, as he told me the little girl was his own daughter.

After a while the mill stopped having company picnics and instead gave each employee a booklet with "wonderful expensive gifts." It began a few weeks before Christmas. One year he got a beautiful barbecue stand and another year a beautiful set of large socket wrenches. There were cameras, Corning Ware and other household items to choose from. "Of course only one item!" he said.

After interviewing Huck, I could see that he had an excellent knowledge of the mill operations, and also that he enjoyed his work and the people. As he spoke to me, his excitement was contagious and he made every effort to help me understand the process. It was as if he were right there in the mill at that very moment. I knew I did not have to ask if he enjoyed his mill experiences, but I did anyway. "Oh very much so! I loved every minute of it," he replied. His wife Jenny added, "It was a paycheck and it helped get the children through college."

As our interview ended, Huck shared with me that he has always had an interest in art. He has a wood shop in his basement where he does crafts. He showed me several birdhouses with paintings of many songbirds representing our area. The paintings were all freehand and beautifully done.

One birdhouse portrayed water birds to which he added a little humor. "There's an eagle and its eggs. A blue heron is looking at the eggs and the eagle is nervously keeping his eye out for the blue heron." He also showed me birdhouses with a wood duck, a loon with its babies, a kingfisher, and a sea gull on them. It is clear that Huck is proud of his work.

He also has made miniature outhouses as gifts for his family. Some of them are for decoration, while some actually hold toilet paper. His attention to humorous detail is apparent in each outhouse and Huck made sure I noticed each one.

His good sense of humor is obvious. "It's a family trait," his wife said. With our son and daughter, we like to do playful family things." And what could be more fun than that!

# James Soter

"Stevens was the best place I ever worked," Jim said. After the mill closed, I worked at Scott & Williams and Webster Valve and they paid more. But Stevens was like a family. They didn't push you."

Born in Franklin on October 4, 1924, Jim grew up on Glen Street. He was drafted into the army in 1943 and served three years. After passing the physical, he had twenty-one days before he had to leave for duty.

On one of those days, he and some of his buddies went swimming at the Webster Lake town beach in Franklin. While there, they decided to swim to the one and only island on the lake. They arrived safely on the island, but then it got windy with high waves and they were afraid to return. They could see a man on shore and shouted to him to bring a boat, but he did not hear them. Finally, they decided to swim back, and all the while he hoped he would not drown, because people would think he committed suicide because he did not want to go into the army. But he said, "We made it back all right."

Jim began at the Franklin mill in 1942 at age eighteen, a year before he went into the army. "There were four of us and we washed every single window in that mill," he said. He has no idea how many windows there were, but it took them all summer long to accomplish the task!

When he returned from the army, he was hired at the mill again and worked nights for a while on the shear, napping the cloth. Before long, a new man came on board who was assigned to the day shift. Jim went to the boss and complained that he had been there longer, and then he was placed on days. While moving from nights to days was common, Jim said it was possible that someone with less seniority could move ahead of you "if you didn't pay attention and complain!" He worked at the mill for twenty-eight years and nine months.

While Jim was working on the shear, he learned that the machines' fixer was about to retire. The fixer's assistant probably would have taken over the job, but he had been injured in a serious accident at the mill. Since Jim had helped to grind the machines at times and had some experience, he was offered the job.

It took all day to grind a machine. Grinding was accomplished by sharpening the blades with emery and oil. "The blade had eight or ten spirals and the blade had to go backwards in order to grind it," Jim said. "Because of the sharp blades, people sometimes lost the tip of a finger if they tried to pull the cloth too closely. They say a fixer often loses a finger, but I was lucky."

Jim was responsible for keeping twenty-six machines running. If any of them broke down, it was his job to fix them. Some of the machines that he took care of were sponges, decaters and presses. He was the only fixer and was responsible for three shifts. If something broke down at night, he was called to come in and fix it. "Sometimes I might be called once a week and other times I don't even use a wrench!" he said. No matter how long the repairs took, whether it was five hours or five minutes, he got two hours overtime.

"If something didn't break down, I could go all week long and do nothing." I thought that would be rather boring and questioned whether he really did just walk around and do nothing. It was so unlike the constant work schedule everyone else seemed to have. His response was that he had a little cubby hole where all the parts were kept and he could go there. Frank, the second hand (his assistant) and sometimes the boss, Mickey Brassard, would join him. "Mickey was a fixer once and he was the one who taught me the job."

Jim said that he, Frank, Alfie Fleury, and the electrician used to cook hamburgers and pork chops for dinner with an electric frying pan in his cubby hole. One day the superintendent came in and said, "We can smell pork chops all over the plant." From then on, they had to put the pan outside on the window sill!

With some pride, Jim told me how a few times he was able to fix a problem quickly that others thought was going to hold up the machines for a long time, or that simply could not be repaired. He still remembers a wonderful compliment he overheard the boss telling another superintendent. "If other fixers are the best in the state, then Jim must be the best fixer in the world!" "It made me feel good," Jim said.

All the shears were equipped with meters. Jim told me a story about a man on a four-blader, as he called it. "He fooled the boss; he fooled them all!" It seemed to others that he just hung around and did not do much work, but his yardage was way up every time someone checked up on him. Jim said they found out he had disconnected the roll where the yardage meter was connected and attached a heavy string on a roll that went fast, which made the meter increase the yardage. "He did that for months," Jim said. "He'd get about 25,000 yards in eight hours." I said I thought it was strange that it went on for so long, but Jim replied, "They believed the machine!" After it was discovered, Jim put a wire around the meters so they could not be tampered with.

Shortly before the mills' closing in 1970, Jim jokingly told a superintendent's son that the mill was not going to be there much longer. The next day the superintendent questioned him, wondering why he had said that to his son, and told Jim the mill had made $2,000,000 in profit that year just from the finishing department. "Of course the mill did close soon after!" Jim said. When it closed, he helped take down the machinery, which was shipped to other Stevens' mills.

Jim enjoyed being on the mill bowling team and was a good bowler. He took the high average, high triple, and high single all in one year. His many trophies are displayed in his living room.

Although it was only February when I visited, Jim had many tomato and pepper plants already started in flats around his apartment. He said he has always loved gardening, but because he lives alone, he gives away most of his bounty.

He also enjoys fishing and goes with friends. He seems to have many friends and much of his free time is spent talking and visiting with them. I asked if they fished for trout and he said, "We fish for anything as long as we catch something." They throw the fish back in, but I gathered that catching something is important! Laughing, he told me he even caught a turtle once—by the foot!

Jim has been married and has a son, but he now lives alone, except for his beautiful Himalayan cat that slept near us on a chair. Jim had mentioned the cat several times as we talked. He pointed out its brown face, brown legs, and its tail with soft angora-like fur. He said it was not really his cat, but whenever he went out, it kept following him home. Even though he lets it out, it pleases him that the cat always returns to his house. When I was ready to leave, Jim picked the cat up and carried him in his arms to the door as we said goodbye.

# Leopold (Paul) Pouliot

At the urging of Jim Soter whom I had interviewed in the morning, I continued on to Paul's house. Jim had spoken with Paul earlier in the day and told him he would send me over after my visit was finished. Considering that I usually called ahead of time to arrange an interview, Paul and his wife, Jill, were most gracious when I just sort of arrived on their doorstep.

Paul was born in Franklin in 1913. He grew up in Franklin and still lives there. He and Jill have three daughters and two sons. He worked for three years at Stevens Franklin Mill, beginning in 1951 at the age of thirty-eight. From there, he went to Lakeport for six years for a better paying job and then to Stevens Tilton Mill for ten years. Paul's wife said he started working in Sulloway Mill when he was only thirteen. In all, he worked fifty-eight years. "Long enough!" Paul said.

He worked all the different shifts. His first job was in wet finish. He said they needed a man to operate the soapers and he had more experience than the other two men, so he was put in charge. "I worked there a year, until I got soap poisoning. I had big red blotches on my hands and all the way up to my elbows. It was a big machine and in the process of treating the cloth they used a lot of chemicals." From wet finish he went upstairs to the dry finish department. "The material came from other mills and we had to process it."

In Tilton, Paul worked in the grey room. He and other workers had to maneuver all the warps. "It was heavy work. The material weighed from 600 to 800 pounds."

When Paul first started working, huge extractors removed the water from the cloth, much like a giant spinner washer. Someone told him the story of how a cat had been hanging around the mill and one man thought it would be funny to put the cat in the extractor. After a few seconds of spinning, they stopped the machine and all they could find were a few hairs. Paul said, "That's how fast that thing went around!"

Another tale involved a boss that no one liked very well. "We were working nights and we were having a cigarette break. We could see these little mice running around and decided to play a little joke on this guy. One guy got on one side of the room and followed the mice. I got at the other end with a paper bag and a mouse went into it. So we put the paper bag in the boss's lunch box. When he opened it up there was a great big yip!"

Paul said he always kind of enjoyed working in the mill. "We had a good bunch and it was a challenge."

He is a member of the Knights of Columbus. He also likes gardening and raising flowers. Laughing, he said, "That gets a little harder every year."

Before I left, Jill and Paul wanted to show me their wedding picture which their children had blown up for their fiftieth wedding anniversary. There were also pictures of their children, grandchildren and great-grandchildren. With pictures everywhere, it is obvious that family is very important to this couple.

# Edward Plizga

Ed began working summers, 3 P.M. to 11 P.M., at the Franklin mill when he was in still in high school. He worked stripping bobbins. Ed's father, and his mother for a while, both worked at Stevens Mill. His father was a loom fixer and worked at the mill almost until the day he died.

As Ed and his two brothers were growing up, they and their mother took care of the family farm. They sold milk to Ed's maternal uncle at the Franklin Dairy, owned by the Kulacz family.

"We worked on the farm seven days a week, before we went to school, and after we came home from school," Ed said. "First thing we had to do was our work!" I asked Ed if he resented working so hard and he said that maybe he did early on, but when he went into the service he learned what respect was. "There's no respect today." I questioned how he could work in the mill and work on the farm, too, and he said, "You just did."

Born on November 17, 1926, Ed said he was raised in Franklin, and except for his service years, he never lived anywhere else. He was drafted into the army in 1945 right after high school. He served two years of active duty in the infantry and fifteen years in the reserves. I suggested that being in the infantry must have been hard, but Ed replied that he did not mind it. "I was made acting squadron leader right off the bat, because I was a farm boy, not a city boy, and I could take anything!"

When Ed came back from the service in 1947, he worked in the mill again. He began in the burling room, then he stripped bobbins, and from there he went to the weave room. When the weave room shut down in Franklin, he went to the Tilton mill. He still has ringing in his ears from the noise of the weave room.

Ed said, "I made good money as a weaver. All three shifts worked by a clock. The clock was set for the first shift and when the second shift came on, it was turned on for that shift, and then for the third shift. The paycheck varied because there were some things the worker had no control over. If the warp had too many ends tied, it broke, and if the yarn was not spun enough, it pulled apart, and the loom would stop. Then the clock would stop, and you wouldn't be making any money. You had to keep those looms pumping! If you had a good warp, you got good money, and if you had a bad warp, you didn't make such good money."

Because they worked so hard in and out of the mill, Ed said sometimes he and the fellow he worked with would fall asleep—but not at the same time! They each had four machines and would help each other to keep the looms running while they had their little cat naps.

"Oh yes," Ed replied when I asked him if he enjoyed working in the mill. "And everyone got along really well." I asked him what he did not like and he said, "I loved it. I had nothing against Stevens Mill."

As if his years of hard work on the farm, in the factory, and extra jobs were not enough, Ed still had time to belong to a number of organizations. He is a life member of the VFW, as well as the Disabled American Veterans and the Elks Club. He belongs to the Legion and the International Police Association of the United States.

He likes to hunt and fish. Responding to my question concerning hobbies, he told me he loves to go up into the woods to cut wood, and because he enjoys it so much, wondered if it was a hobby. I assured him it was!

In spite of health problems which have slowed him down considerably, Ed still lives in his own home, which he says he built himself from oak trees cut on his parents' property. Although twice married, Ed now lives alone. When I commented on how clean and beautiful his house is, he said that he takes care of it all by himself!

# Ethel and James* Magoon

"Stevens Mill gave Christmas parties in December and held outings during the summer," Ethel said. "We'd bring the whole family, kids and all, and it was great! Everybody had such a good time."

Jim remembered the outings at Bear Brook State Park. "One year I caught a pig. They greased a pig and I caught it!" Jim also remembered a Christmas that was not so great, when the company did not have enough money to give everyone a gift, and gave each worker an apple as a token gift!

Ethel and Jim Magoon both worked in the Franklin mill. Ethel was born in 1920 in Portsmouth, then moved to Dover where she went to school. She moved to Tilton with her mother in 1938. "That is where I met my handsome husband Jim," she said. After dating for three years, they married and moved to Franklin. The couple has been in Franklin ever since. They have three children: twin daughters and a son.

Jim was born in Franklin, also in 1920, and grew up in West Franklin. He attended the Nesmith School and is an army veteran of World War II.

Ethel started working at the mill in 1958 or 1959, and worked in the sales and services office until the mill closed. Describing her job, she said, "We worked on big ledgers. We quoted all the goods that came into the mill and the departments they went to, right up until they were finished and shipped out."

I asked if she liked her job. "Oh very much, we had a nice group of

* *Died July 2, 2000*

people. Bill Fisher was the head of the office. He was very nice. Bill always made you feel comfortable. He was a good business man, but he was full of the dickens, you know."

I told Ethel that when I interviewed Bill, he told me he hired people. When I asked if he also fired people, he told me he did not. Ethel quickly replied, "Nobody ever got fired!"

Jim started working at the mill around 1943. He worked there for twenty-nine years. He explained his job this way. "When I first began working, I worked in the card room for quite a while. In the card room, we took raw material and ground it up to make roping. The cards thinned the material right out to its proper thickness. Then the yarn went on spools." Later, he worked in the shipping and sample division of the mill.

"The machines were noisy, but we were still able to tell jokes—some dirty—and fool around at times," he said. "Often, someone at the top of the stairs would drop water onto a guy below and they wouldn't know who it was. Some of the things we did were probably foolish, but at the time they seemed pretty funny." I commented that of course they were young and with the long days in the mill, they probably needed those distractions, and he agreed.

While accidents were not common, Jim did observe one accident in the card room. "A foreman upstairs in the card room got his hand caught in the machine and lost part of his hand." When I said I would probably write about the accident without naming the person, Jim said he did not care. "I'm the type of person—I don't care, I don't lie, I tell the truth!"

Overtime was very important. Jim said they had all the overtime they wanted, remarking, "If they paid more money we probably wouldn't have needed overtime." Overtime was time and a half.

Jim carried his lunch in a dinner pail. He said the big black pails kept the food fairly warm or cool. He mentioned also that some children brought their fathers' lunches to them at work. Ethel said some of the wives, who were at home and not working, prepared a hot meal and sent the hot food with the children for their fathers to eat.

"The truth of it was," Jim said, "the French people, who lived from River Street down through that section as far up as Prospect Hill, the men were boss of the family. They wanted their dinner hot!

"If the kids worked, they went home and gave all their money to their parents and, of course, at that time they needed the money! Then the parents gave it out with the idea that they use it right or they don't get it, which is a good thing. If the kids would only pay attention to their grandparents today, they'd have more money when they retire."

Jim enjoyed working in the mill. "Everyone was agreeable," he said. "We all worked together. I really liked it for the simple reason that you had all kinds of people there and we all got used to it. We had fights, you know what I mean, but not that bad. Every once in a while we lost our tempers, but the next morning we were happy. Even she and I, we've been married for fifty-seven years, and we can't always agree.

Co-workers were definitely considered friends. Ethel said they have stayed that way ever since the mill shut down. While many have died, she keeps in touch with others, and does things with women she used to work with.

The mill had bowling leagues, for both men and women, and baseball teams. Jim played baseball. "In the mill there were two Soter boys and one of them, Ted Soter, for goodness sakes, was a champion from the state of New Hampshire!" The mill also held end-of-the-season banquets and gave out trophies to the different teams.

There was one benefit of working in the mill that Jim really liked. When gabardine material was first made, it was very expensive. Some of the bosses bought gabardine pants that would have cost eighty-nine dollars in stores and sold them to the workers for twenty dollars. Ethel also liked the fact that she could buy material at the mill to make clothes.

Jim mentioned Jim Horman, a superintendent at the Tilton mill in the sixties, and what a nice man he is. "You can tell with those older people, they were strict with what they did, but they had feelings for other people. Today nobody has feelings. That was a good feature about living back in those times, we had feelings for everybody."

Jim said Stevens was a good place to work. "It was the best place in Franklin to work. They paid more than a lot of places." Ethel responded by saying that back then if you had a job, you kept it to the end, not like now when you're never sure of your job. "The mill was like family. You could talk about problems and they'd help you out."

One of Ethel's interests was ceramics. She took painting classes first and then took classes in ceramics. Soon she had her own business teaching ceramics. Jim proudly said she had made everything in the house. Ethel said, "I made a lot of things; I've given a lot away." Laughing she said, "I've made so much for the kids they don't want anymore." Jim showed me many of her beautiful pieces throughout the house including a milk can, jugs, dishes and much more, attesting to Ethel's talent.

In addition to his many hours of work at Stevens, Jim was active in the Franklin community. For several years he served as a call fireman for the city, as well as three terms as a city councilor. He was a life member of the Veterans of Foreign Wars. He also enjoyed snowmobiling, hunting and fishing, and was active in area sports.

Over the years Ethel and Jim enjoyed traveling to Maine each summer for vacation.

# Gloria Crosby

Gloria was a classmate of mine at Franklin High School where she was a popular student and a cheerleader. It was a joy to meet her again, and to try to catch up on the intervening years.

She was born on November 3, 1929 in Sanford, Maine, where her grandparents had come from Canada to work in the Sanford Mill. They came by train with their thirteen children, specifically to work in the mill. Gloria's family moved to Franklin when she was four months old, so she considers herself a Franklinite. She attended school and lived in Franklin until she and her husband, Ken, moved across the town line to Tilton fifteen years ago, for smaller living quarters.

Gloria began her first Stevens job at the Franklin mill in 1948, a year after she graduated from high school, and worked until she married in 1950. She worked in the weave room "dropping wires." On a huge frame, every piece of thread was separated by a long thin wire that was dropped into a space onto the loom. She said, "You went from one loom to another all day long." During that period she also did other jobs that were assigned to her.

In 1952, when her son was eighteen months old, she went to the Tilton mill and worked as a frame spinner. She planned to work for two or three years, but worked there for eighteen years, until it closed. "I wanted a job where I didn't have to go far from home and just something to help out. I didn't care what I did." she said.

The first three years, Gloria worked second shift and then went to the day shift. She had earned ninety cents an hour with her very first job in the mill. But as a spinner she was paid by the piece. She worked with a partner, each having three frames. She said you could make more money that way. "We did pretty good. It was good for the times and it was extra money for us."

Gloria said, "Frame spinning involved three huge machines with three big spools on each frame with about sixty bobbins on one side and sixty on the other. You had to drop those down in the frame, tie the ends, and let them spin up. Then you had to doff (take the bobbins off), put new bobbins on, and start all over again." About ten people, both men and women, worked in the spinning room. It was very noisy, but not as noisy as the weave room. "Those people must be all stone deaf today!" she said.

Gloria thought piecework was measured by the number of spools the spinner put in, the amount of doffing done, and how much yarn was taken off the frame. But she was not sure how it was figured out, because the worker did not have to do it. It was done automatically with a clock. She said spinning was very hard work for a woman, but a lot of women did it, because it paid pretty well, especially if you could work fast.

Frame spinners were not supposed to shut down their machines to eat lunch. They had to continue working while they ate. Gloria said that was not right, because sometimes work was so hard they did not have time to eat. "You couldn't do that today!" Often, some of the wool on the frame was nubby and terrible to work with and it would break and need to be retied. Some bosses were not understanding. She said, "If you can imagine three of those huge machines with the ends breaking all the time. See, when you put that spool down in the frame, you had to connect it to the thread that was coming up from the bobbin, and sometimes when you got them all in they would break—a lot! If there were too many breaks, the machine would stop. It was a hard job!"

At one time, she had a difficult boss who came by when she had two frames shut down, because she was so hungry she had to eat. He said, "What are you doing sitting down?" She replied, "I'm sitting down, because I'm hungry and you are not going to stop me. If you want to run these, you start them up and you run them, and if you have any complaints I'll go to the boss, because I'm going to eat!" She said he never bothered her after that.

Working on the frames was such hard work that as she grew older she was tired after working just six hours to say nothing of eight. When the mill closed, Gloria said it was really one of the best things that ever happened to her. Not that it was a good thing for everyone, but for her it was.

She said the mill had health insurance, but no sick days. If a day was missed, there was no pay. Vacation was two weeks with six holidays.

From time to time, she said comical things happened and gave this example. There were steel trucks near their spinning frames with a stepboard in front of them. Someone would come by to pick up the full bobbins they had doffed and put them in the trucks. One day she and her girlfriend were waiting for one of the spools to run down (called a home run). If they did not wait, it had to be done all over again by hand and it was lots of work. While they waited, they sat on the edge of a truck with their feet on the stepboard. As they were talking, the truck slipped and they fell into it and could not get out. They laughed and laughed, and when the young man came to pick up the bobbins, he asked what had happened. They shouted, "We fell in. Help us out!"

Like so many other people, Gloria said "working at the mill was a job," and she was grateful to have it. She went to work to pay for extras, not to have a career. Once she started working, she wanted to continue, because she and her husband were getting ahead. She went on to say, "I enjoyed the people. The people were very nice."

Reflecting further, she said, "I did the best with what I had to do. I had a job and I earned my money honestly. I worked hard for it and I don't owe anybody a thing and I'm content."

Last year at age sixty-nine, with the urging of her husband, Gloria bought her first car, just for herself. Laughing heartily, she told me her son had said, "Ma, honest, I don't believe you. You started skiing at thirty-two, you took up golf at sixty-five, and you're getting a car at sixty-nine!"

Today she loves playing cards, reading, skiing, and playing golf every chance she gets. She also walks and exercises. Her youthful appearance attests to her healthy life style.

Gloria said that in all the years she was working she never had time to go out and do things, but now, "I'm really enjoying myself, and that's all that matters!"

# Richard (Woody) Woodward

"The mill contributed to a lot of the pollution in the river," Woody said. "We dumped everything into the river. All the soap suds, carbon tetrachloride from the carbonizer, chemicals from the dye kettles, the whole nine yards, and I think that was one of the main reasons the mill closed." Worrying about the environment did not come until later, but Woody thinks the company could see it coming and wanted to get out while they could.

I met Richard and his wife, Laura, on a rainy day in June at their home on the New Hampton Road. He assured me right away that "Nobody knows me by anything but Woody."

He was born in Franklin on October 29, 1925, "right up the road from where we live now." He and his wife have five children. Laura was born in Louisiana, but has felt right at home in Franklin and thinks she was meant to be a New Englander. Woody was not in the military because he had a handicapped brother to support, as well as his mother.

He began at Stevens in Franklin between 1943 and 1944, and worked until almost the time of closing. He started in the maintenance department, where he worked for less than a year for Mr. Blake, who was the boss of the department. From there, he went to firing the boilers for three or four years. Then he was transferred back to the maintenance department to set up and maintain machinery. "I worked on dryers, carbonizer, everything in wet and dry finish."

When he worked in the engine room, the first thing they did in the morning was rake the racks to keep the garbage out of the water in the river. "That was so the water wheels wouldn't starve for water. If there was no water in the water wheel, there was no power," he said. They also washed the filters down every morning.

Woody said he worked crazy hours when he was firing the boilers with coal. They changed shifts every week. "Every other weekend we'd have a twelve hour shift on days and the second weekend a twelve hour shift at night. It spoiled your weekends. But hey, it was a good job and it paid well for the area.

"We had three big HRT (Horizontal Return) boilers and one combustion boiler. With coal, we kept losing the steam, because the load was so heavy. When the boiler ran out of steam, the engine would shut down, and that shut down much of the mill. The engine would stay shut down until the steam was running and then they'd go along again." After Woody left the department, the mill changed to oil for fuel, and oil made the job much easier.

His main job in maintenance was to set up machines. However, if something was broken he had to leave what he was doing to fix the breakdown. He worked days but was on twenty-four hour call. If something broke down at night he was called in, and if extra help was needed, he called someone else to come in, too. "My last boss there was George Jurta—a prince of a gentleman—a nice smart foreman," he said.

Woody said there was a lot of lifting on the job and that working on the machines was hard on his back. He had a couple of ruptures while he was there, which he said, very nonchalantly, he had "fixed." Working on the machines was also very hot work. "The temperature in the machines was unbelievable. You could hardly hold your hand on the floor. We had to keep the machines running because if the cloth stayed in the hot machine too long it would be damaged." Yet, after all that, he still said, "It was a very good job.

"Dust and smoke from the coal was awful. Coal was very dirty. Of course we breathed the coal dust all day, but we just never thought about it being dangerous. The boiler room was really hard work. We worked continuously there. Definitely harder than working on the machines."

Woody said when he was working on the boilers there was never any time that he was not working. "But if the boss came around when I was working on the machines, and I was sitting down, the boss would be tickled to death, because that was a good sign. It meant all the machines were running!" Nonetheless, they still had their projects to do, too, such as making guards and "stuff" for the machines.

At first, he could not think of anything when I questioned if there was anything he did not like about working in the mill. His wife commented, "It was a way of life. We took all the unpleasant things with the good things and gave nothing a priority."

I could sense Woody wanted to add something, but was hesitant. Then he remarked, "With twenty-five to thirty people in maintenance—the carpenters, the pipe fitters, and so many others—I guess there was some jealousy." He added, "You get friction anywhere. You can't help it."

He thinks the reason others may have been jealous of him was because he was the one called if something broke down. Woody knew what to look for, because he had experience with lathe work, welding, and all aspects of maintenance. He could go in and get the machinery running without needing to call in half the people, because he had repaired breakdowns for so long. "I got a lot of overtime and made real good money!

"But I worked a lot of hours," Woody said. He often put in fifty, sixty, seventy, even eighty hours a week. "When they called me, I would go in to work. Some others would either not come in or would not answer the phone. They never called me but what I didn't go. Sometimes foremen from other departments would call me, because they couldn't get their own people to come in. I figure if you can't get a person when you need him, then he is not much good to you. My family is that way. We are dedicated."

As we sat talking Woody added, "It was hard getting a job at Stevens, because everyone wanted to work there and it was the best paying job around. Probably the hourly rate wasn't that good, but the overtime made it good." Once again he remarked, "It was a good place to work. You had a few bad knocks like you do anywhere. There was no perfect job, but that was as near as you could get!"

He had an inkling that the mill might close three or four months before it did. His wife added that he had a little inside knowledge because Foster Blue, a superintendent, was a hunting partner. Woody said when bosses from Stevens' southern mills started checking in, he could see the handwriting on the wall.

He agreed to start a job with the New England Telephone company not long before the mill closed. The company had been after him to go to work for them for three or four years, but because of all his mill overtime pay he would have started for less pay than at the mill. But seeing the possibility that the mill might close, it seemed like the right thing to do. After working at the telephone company for a while, he made good pay there, too. Woody said the mill closing really did him a favor, but that many people never recovered from it and he felt bad for them. His wife said, "So many people thought they were there for life."

Woody did not belong to any organizations, because he said he just was not that kind of a person. "I was a loner." When I asked if he had hobbies, his quick reply was "fishing and hunting." He took his children with him. He and his wife do a lot of traveling. They have a motor home and use it to go down South. They also fly many places and have traveled out West, and every year they visit a daughter in Colorado. On weekends they like to take trips around the area.

# Yvonne* and Roger Desrochers

"You never get used to working nights, but what are you going to do?" Roger said. "You worked your way down to days and you might get it, if you lived to be a hundred years old!" The hours worked depended on the kind of work, but while he was weaving, Roger never worked days.

Roger was born in 1924. He began working at Stevens Mill in Franklin in 1942, right out of high school. In 1943, he joined the Marine Corps and served for three years. Upon discharge, he resumed working at Stevens, and in all, worked a total of twenty-four years for the company.

Most of the time he did weaving. While he was learning to weave, he worked two weeks for no pay. He said, "People wouldn't do that today." I asked if weaving was the hardest job, and Roger responded, "It was the best paying job. When you made a dollar an hour in those days, you were doing pretty good."

Roger explained what he did as a weaver. "You just kept the machine going. If the yarn broke, the machine automatically stopped, so you retied the knot and started it up again. The bobbins dropped into the shuttle automatically. When the bobbin got way down in the shuttle, there was a mechanism to trip it from the magazine, and that dropped another bobbin into the shuttle and you just kept going.

"You kept those machines going and when you got seventy or eighty yards on a bolt of cloth, you had to take it off and put an empty roll down

---

* *Died June 23, 2001*

and start the cloth winding up again. The cloth was about fifty-five inches wide, and when it was all wound up, you probably had seventy or eighty yards. But you wouldn't do that in one shift, oh no! Somebody else would take over. You put a tag in the cloth with your name on it. If something's wrong they know who to give hell to." We all laughed and Yvonne, who had been awaiting her turn said, "That's how they know your piecework."

Roger went on to explain piecework. "You got paid so much a yard. A yard was a thousand picks. When that machine went a thousand times, the cloth gave one turn. That's how we got paid. One pick was one turn or one shuttle across. You took the clock readings and kept it until the end of the week, then you knew how much money you should make." I was surprised that weavers were trusted to keep track of their own time, but he said timekeepers kept track, too. Each department had an office. The office girl came around to read the clock, and "you wanted to check them to make sure they were doing it right!"

He ate his lunch while he was working. He said he did not have a lunch hour. He also had no breaks while he was weaving. "Take your break and you're losing money!

Working in the weave room was very noisy, but Roger said when you are working, you get used to it. I commented that if it was noisy they probably couldn't talk, tell jokes, or fool around. He said, "Oh no, we were there to work!" But Yvonne interrupted and said, "Oh, they did!"

Roger was working 11 P.M. to 7 A.M. and then got laid off weaving, because a lot of the older weavers were going from Franklin to Tilton. "So I had to carry the filler for a while. Fillers are bobbins that fit in the shuttle to weave the cloth, and you carry that to the looms and put them in boxes."

Other jobs Roger had when he was not weaving were time study, loom inspection, and checking for yarn breaks on the looms, as well as working in the spinning room. He said he worked all over. When they switched all the picking, carding, spinning, and weaving to Tilton, he went there.

The mill had a safety committee with people serving from different departments. Members walked through the plant once a month checking to make sure there were no safety hazards. Roger was the safety director at the Tilton mill. He said Liberty Mutual Insurance set up the safety programs. "They wanted to make sure we didn't have any accidents to take money from the insurance company. They had a method to their madness!" he said.

Yvonne worked at the Franklin mill in the downstairs office. She gave a brief description of her work. "I started out doing the inventory, every piece of cloth on a card, and I followed it all the way through the mill." The job was supposed to be for only six weeks, but then she was asked to take the job permanently. Her son was only six months old and she was not looking for a full-time position, but she decided to accept it. Eventually, she worked with Ralph Manchester in the sample office.

Yvonne recounted how the mill had Christmas parties and summer barbecues that everyone attended, and she remembered going to Gunstock Recreation Area and the fun of going on rides. They also went to Bear Brook State Park. There were games for the children, as well as the adults. "I was conned into a three-legged race once. Everyone had a good time!"

Roger said most of the workers got along together. "Yeah, in those days, they probably wouldn't today." He enjoyed working in the mill, but said people did not have much choice, because "there was no other place to work." Yvonne said she liked working in the mill very much.

Roger was a city councilman for nine years and Yvonne said it was probably easier then than it would be now, because there were not as many confrontations. Roger said he never really had any hobbies and that just taking care of a home had kept him busy. Once in a while he worked on his car. And sometimes he played golf, but he said, "I wasn't an addict. I didn't have to play golf!" When he was a boy, he caddied.

Roger and Yvonne have a son and a daughter. The couple has enjoyed traveling to Florida and the Grand Canyon. They also attend some of the Marine reunions and said they have a good time.

It may not be a hobby but Roger and a few other men (my brother included) meet at McDonald's for coffee every morning. My sisters and I like to kid my brother by saying, "They meet to solve all the world's problems." Let us hope they can!

# Jean Carignan

Jean was hanging out some clothes on a warm mid-March day when I arrived at her house on Central Street. She said it was the first time since fall that she had hung anything outside, "and it felt so good."

Jean was born in Franklin on May 8, 1927, in the house where she still lives on Willow Hill. After graduating from high school, she worked in Concord for four years. She returned to Franklin and began working in the weave room office at Stevens Mill in 1949, when she was twenty-two years old. She married her husband, Maurice, (now deceased) in 1950. Maurice was a quiller fixer at the mill.

"Weaving, spinning, carding, drawing-in, and quilling moved from Franklin to the Tilton plant in 1950," Jean said. She added that in the beginning, the mill wanted two people from each shift to go to Tilton, before moving the whole crew there from those departments. Some of the newer people got the better jobs, because the old-timers didn't want to move. When it came time that they had to, they had to take whatever job was available. She said, "They just thought it wouldn't happen, I guess." Jean, also, went to Tilton in 1950, and worked until 1954.

During 1955 and 1956, Jean worked in Franklin again, in the office for Doug Veasey. Then she stayed home with her children, except for some waitressing. In 1964, she tried the mill again and went back to Tilton. But her children were still young, so she only worked for a year.

One of Jean's jobs was to take the clock readings for all three shifts on each loom in the weave room. She took the readings and then set the clocks back. If weavers worked overtime or on weekends, she had to go in then, too, to read and reset the clocks. Another job responsibility was doing the payroll for those who worked in mending, drawing-in, and quilling. She also did efficiency reports.

I questioned whether she thought the weavers were overworked and Jean replied that she did not think so. Even people who did piecework were allowed to work at their own pace. "Some worked like the devil and made the highest money, and some didn't care and took their time. Today if they didn't make their quota they'd be fired, but in those days they just put them on day pay." Jean explained that day pay meant an hourly wage.

Jean was working at the Franklin Savings Bank when the mill closed. She said, "So many people worked in the mill that on Friday nights, they were all lined up at the door to cash their checks. When the mill closed, people were not expecting it, and some—those who were older and especially those with big families to support—were floored."

Over the years Jean has kept very busy with her four children and their families, but she said she likes to knit and crochet. She always wanted to learn how to quilt, and after her husband died, she did learn how. She has made fifty-seven Log Cabin quilts for her children, grandchildren, nieces and nephews, and brothers and sisters. She recently completed a Dresden Plate quilt and says she will never attempt to make another one, because it was so difficult and time consuming. I was delighted to have her show it to me. It is extremely colorful and beautiful, certainly an accomplishment that she can be proud of! I told her that just maybe, she'll make another one someday.

# Kenneth Larrivee

"There's an art to working the third shift," Ken told me, "and that is making sure you get your sleep." He ate breakfast as soon he got home and went to bed right away, getting up around 2 P.M. That way he had all afternoon and evening to himself.

Ken was born in Lisbon, New Hampshire on July 29, 1924. When he was about four years old, his family moved to Laconia. He grew up there, and attended the Laconia schools.

In 1942, he enlisted in the United States Army during World War II, and became a pilot in the army air force. While in the army, he was a pilot instructor and taught classes for the Free French Air Force members, who had escaped from France. "They found out I spoke French, so that's where they put me," Ken said. I told Ken I had not interviewed a pilot before. He laughed and said, "Well, now you have!"

After three and a half years in the service, he went to work at the Scott and Williams Mill in Laconia. That's where he met his wife, Loda, who was also working there. Soon they moved to Franklin, which was her hometown. They have three daughters and a son.

Ken began working in dry finish on the first shift at the Franklin mill in 1951, when he was twenty-seven years old. He worked nineteen years altogether, until the mill closed in 1970.

After his first year at the mill, there was an opening for a third shift supervisor in dry finish. Ken took the job and worked the third shift, 11 P.M. to 7 A.M., for the rest of his time at Stevens. He said, however, that sometimes in the winter when business was slow, the mill would combine the second and third shifts, and he and the second shift supervisor worked on the second shift together.

As supervisor, Ken was in charge of the dry finish process, which followed wet finish. He had about fifteen employees working for him. "What

I had to do," he said, "was assign the work and look at the quality of their product when they finished. With three shifts, work just continued from one shift to the next, each one picking up where the other shift left off. After dry finish, the cloth went to perching to be inspected, and then to shipping."

Shearing and pressing were in the dry finish room, too. "The shears were like big lawn mowers that the cloth went through to clip it all even. A powerful suction pulled up most of the lint, but there was some lint flying around the room." Ken never felt it was unhealthy, not to him anyway. He thinks the workers cleaned and swept up their own areas, eliminating the need for janitors.

He ate his lunch in his office, while the workers ate near their machines, or wherever they could find a place. Laughing, he said, "After I finished my lunch, I had to take off and look for them, because they'd get sleepy and I'd find them on a bolt of cloth sound asleep!"

As we talked about safety, Ken said there was a nurse on the day shift, but on second and third shifts the supervisors were responsible for first aid. He remembered only one person he had to take to the hospital, a man who really only lost some skin off his hand.

Summer was the busiest time of the year and Ken said they had to work six days a week. The only thing he remembered not liking about his job was going into work Sunday night in the summer, because it was so hot. He said, "All the windows were closed Saturday, so the cloth wouldn't get wet in case it rained. Most of the machines in dry finish operated by steam and it would be 140 and 150 degrees when I went in there!" He said it was really bad until they could get the windows opened to cool it off.

Ken's boss, the first shift supervisor, was responsible for all three shifts. One night as Ken was going through one of the rooms upstairs he said, "This bat came zooming from one end to the other. I grabbed the broom and had a lucky shot and put him out of his misery. So I put it in the boss's desk drawer. That morning he opened the drawer and came screaming out of his office and everyone laughed like heck."

Ken had another story for me in which Stevens people were involved. He said he was not a hunter, but Mickey Brassard talked him into going hunting one time with a couple of other Stevens men—Foster Blue, the superintendent of the whole mill, and Alan Milnes. "After they had parked the car, Mickey told me to go down the road a ways and there would be a big pasture, and maybe a big deer would be there. The three guys left me to go in another direction. When I got to the pasture, sure enough, there was a deer. I said to myself, 'Oh my God, there's a deer over there.' I started shooting and emptied my gun. All the guys came running, wondering what was happening. I told them, 'The damn deer won't fall down.'" The guys started laughing and laughing. The "deer" was made of cardboard, and his friends were the ones who had put it there to play a trick on him.

Ken was a city councilman for three years during the time he was working at Stevens. He named others who served at the same time: Bill Fisher, Charlie Pierce and Bob Dorman. If some of the meetings ran after 11 P.M., as the meetings sometimes could, they were allowed to arrive late at their jobs. He said Stevens was very good about it and very civic-minded. "Of course with the company being in Franklin, they had a real interest in what was happening in the city, and how it would affect the mill." Ken also is a member of the Knights of Columbus.

I asked Ken if he thought the mill's closing was a big shock to the employees. He answered, "There was always talk, but everyone said no one could duplicate our dyeing process and they didn't have the water from the river. But then zoom! And just like that, they went!" After the mill closed, he worked for the city of Franklin.

While we talked, Ken's very active, playful kitten kept us entertained as she rattled my papers, jumped on the furniture, and ran around our legs.

Building models is Ken's hobby. He enjoys making airplane models, of course, and does boat models as well. He showed me his large Miss Winnipesaukee Chris Craft model that is in the living room, and told me about building the old Mount Washington Cruise Boat, which he has in his basement. With a smile, he said, "I have enjoyed my hobby."

# George Sargent

*George Sargent, 1965*

When George was a child, he went from school to the mill at lunch time, to eat lunch with his mother and father. While there, he also often spent time with his grandfather who worked in the weave room. George played with some of his grandfather's tools and sometimes even started up the loom. "You wouldn't be able to do that today," he said. "It would be against the law now, but I was indoctrinated into the mill at an early age. It came kind of natural for me."

At his home in Northfield, George met me at the door with a smile. Wearing a green shirt, he is a tallish man with kind eyes, who made me feel comfortable immediately.

He was born in Franklin, New Hampshire on October 3, 1922, and grew up there. During World War II, he joined the Marines and was in the 4th Marine Corps Division. He served in the Marines for thirty-eight months, some of the time in the Pacific battles, with Iwo Jima being one of the last. When I asked if he had been injured, he smiled and said, "No, I was one of the lucky ones."

When George was discharged, he returned to Franklin. He and his wife, Rita, have two daughters and a son. He was twenty-four years old when he began working at the Franklin mill in 1946. He worked there for eight years and then later at the Tilton mill for another sixteen years.

He started in the mending and burling department as a floor boy learning the business. "On Saturdays I'd go in and it was like going to school. I learned the workings of the mill in various departments from the older overseers." After about a year, there was an opening for an overseer in the mending and burling department and George thought the company would hire someone from the North Andover plant. He told the superintendent, Roger Smith—"a heck of a nice guy"—that he was going to go to school on the GI Bill, since it did not appear there was anything at the mill for him.

The superintendent hated to see George leave, saying he was a good worker and that he did a "good job with the ladies." (Mending and burling consisted of all women.) Not thinking he had a chance for advancement, George gave his notice. The next day when he went to work, the superintendent offered to put him on trial as an overseer in the department, if he would like the job. George said that of course he was pleased and accepted the position. After months of running the department, he was put on a salary status.

When the Tilton mill became the manufacturing mill, and the Franklin mill became the finishing mill, George moved to the Tilton mill. He still headed the mending and burling department. This was the last operation of the manufacturing plant before the cloth was shipped to the finishing plant in Franklin to be dyed, finished, and shipped out.

"The women examined the cloth with power perchers," George said. "They were motor-run machines that the cloth ran through, so that imperfections in the cloth could be seen. They had glass front panels with six lights inside. If there were defects, they pulled down on the cloth and fixed it by sewing it in.

*George Sargent with perchers, 1970*

"Before the perchers were motorized, the floor boy had to handle one piece of cloth at a time for the women by putting it on rollers. The women pulled the cloth over two rollers, to look at one side, and then the other side. The power perchers folded the cloth at the same time, making everything a lot faster and easier." Thirty-five to seventy-five women worked in George's department. They had twenty minutes for lunch. That was the state law. But because they were on piecework, some of them ate their lunch while working, to make more money. "They were not pressured, however," George said. "There was a base pay, so if someone wanted to take it easy they could, but they wouldn't make much money!" At one time the women made only eleven cents an hour and he does not know how they lived on that.

There were five departments and five supervisors at the Tilton mill. George said they were all nice guys and they got along well together. Each one tried hard to solve any problems in their respective department. Because he ran a department, he did not get too friendly with his co-workers. He stated, "When you run a department, the boss is the boss, and you can't get too friendly with certain people, because other people would think you're giving them all the best work."

George thought most of the women got along well, but there was some gossiping. "I used to say, 'I could write a book,' but that would not be right." He trained a lot of the women right out of high school and they stayed until the plant shut down. He also worked some days as a supervisor at the North Andover plant and traveled back and forth, with the company paying his expenses.

"The company treated me well," George said. "They had good people working for them." He sees former employees around today and they all say, "We never knew we had it so good. If the plant started up tomorrow we'd come back and work for you." Comments like that make him feel good and he misses it himself.

He, like so many others, said the workers were like one big family. He, too, mentioned the softball teams, company picnics at Gunstock and Bear Brook. "We had some good times!"

George went on to philosophize a bit, "When it comes to a company, they're the ones paying your salary, so the company always comes first. That's the way they taught me. Of course I learned a lot of that stuff in the Marine Corps, so it comes easy to me."

I asked what he liked most about working in the mill and he said, "I liked seeing things that needed to be done and then watching them 'come out.'" He liked the finishing part. He also liked listening to some of the old-timers. "If they liked you, they'd tell you things."

Was there anything he did not like? "I don't really think so. I departed with a good feeling. In my mind I liked the way things were going. I didn't have everything easy, but that's how you learn. And I felt bad when I moved to the Tilton mill from the Franklin mill and couldn't take all of my people with me."

In the past, hardball and softball were George's favorite sports, as well as horseshoes. "I loved horseshoes!" He helped organize some of those sports for the company. However, his main hobby right now is golf. The day of our interview was a beautiful day and I told him I was afraid I was keeping him away from playing golf. Laughing, he said, "Oh no, I played yesterday and the little white ball wouldn't go where I wanted it to go."

After the mill shut down, George worked at Wellington State Park in Bristol for a number of years. Over the years he belonged to the Fourth Marine Division Association, which has its own division in New Hampshire. He is a lifelong member of the VFW and a member of the K of C, as well as the Elks for twenty years.

It appears George was very civic-minded, too. He belonged to the fire department and was an auxiliary policeman. He was also a city councilman. Laughing, he said, "I would get calls at all times of the day and night and often have my supper interrupted, but I didn't care and I enjoyed it."

# Pauline Bergeron

*Pauline Bergeron at the switchboard, at J. P. Stevens, 1969*

Pauline was one of the many LaPlantes in Franklin who my mother always said were our distant cousins. Her grandfather, Eugene LaPlante, mentioned earlier in my father's story, was the cousin my father said was responsible for his family coming to Franklin.

Two of my sisters accompanied me on this interview to discuss our genealogy and found that if we went back far enough, about five generations, we shared the same great-great-grandparents.

Pauline was born in Franklin in 1928, and grew up there. She married her husband, Laurier, in 1947. They have three children. She worked at the local telephone company until it changed to the dial system in 1964.

She then became a switchboard operator at Stevens Mill for six years, until it closed. She worked the day shift, 8 A.M. to 5 P.M., five days a week. Pauline described her job this way. "I was the receptionist and telephone operator which was very interesting. I love telephone work!" She worked on the switchboard all day long. Most day calls were business calls to and from other plants with very few personal calls. There were people who relieved her when she went on break or to lunch.

The other two shifts did not have a switchboard operator. "At night we put up some special connections, so if the phone rang, it would ring in three different places depending on which line it came on." She explained that someone could always be reached if necessary.

At lunch time she went home or out to the main office. "My switchboard was located in a small room within the large personnel office. It had a small lounge. Bill Fisher was personnel officer at the time."

I said I often asked in my interviews if the workers played jokes on each other, talked a lot, or gossiped? Pauline responded with a smile and said, "We did all of that." Then she told me the following story.

"I was the person who gave out change for the vending machines. There was this one guy who worked down in the dye room who smelled something wicked. It must have been years since he bathed. It was kind of disgusting, but it was also kind of comical. Every time Charlie Pierce saw the man coming, Charlie would hurry over and stand there talking just to hold the guy in my room a little longer. One day I said, 'One of these days, Charlie, I'm going to get you.' So I got a can of Lysol Spray and got Charlie with it. He didn't do that again!"

When I asked if she liked working at the mill, Pauline exclaimed, "I loved it! You felt as if you lost your family when it closed." In her off hours, she went bowling and out to eat with her co-workers. She definitely felt they were her friends. When I asked if there was anything she disliked about working at the mill, she thought for a long time before finally saying she could not remember anything.

With her working days behind her, Pauline now generously spends many hours working for Saint Paul's Church, where she is a member.

# Bertrand Deshaies

I traveled to Webster Lake in Franklin to interview Bert on a beautiful October morning with the foliage still in its full glory.

Bert was born in Franklin on September 21, 1929, and has lived there all of his life, except for his service years. He served on three different occasions. The first time, he entered the army in January 1949, and remained for a year. Then after six months as an inactive reservist, he was called back for the Korean War and spent time in Kentucky and Germany. When he was discharged, he began work at Stevens Mill in Franklin and worked there for two or three years.

Bert started work in quality control with Bob Dorman, who trained him for different jobs in the mill. His job in quality control took him into the card room to check the weight of the yarn and into the spinning room to do random checks with four or five bobbins at a time. He took the bobbins off a machine and checked them for strength. In the weave room he checked for defects in the cloth. "If there was a wrong draw where they drew the yarn in, it changed the pattern and you could see it. The weaver would have to fix it," he said. Later, he was sent to the Tilton mill where he worked nights for a while, checking on different departments.

When quality control was discontinued in Tilton, Bert was sent to the Franklin mill again. There, he worked checking swatches of cloth for a variation in shades of color. If there were differences, he notified the dye house and they made corrections.

While he liked quality control because he was more or less his own boss, Bert found checking the swatches rather boring. For that reason, he decided to leave the mill. He enlisted in the air force, this time with the intention of making the service a career. He added, however, that for several reasons he did not.

Bert belongs to the Knights of Columbus, the VFW, the American Legion and the Lockmere Country Club.

Golf is one of his hobbies and he loves the game. During the winter months he likes to do jigsaw puzzles. He also enjoys working around the house.

# Marjorie Terreault

Marjorie and her eight year old cat, Mittens, greeted me at the door when I arrived for our interview. From the moment I entered the house, it was obvious that this beautiful, mostly white cat was indeed an especially loved animal. Marjorie, a widow, said he is definitely her friend and companion in the large house they share. Throughout my stay, she was constantly aware of Mittens' comfort and whereabouts.

Something else which greeted me was the delicious aroma of baked goods. Marjorie had baked cookies and squares for me, as well as a tomato soup cake for her brother. She said that even though she lives alone, she continues to cook and bake for family and friends.

Marjorie was born in Franklin on December 11, 1921, not far from where she now lives. She began working at the Franklin mill in 1951, right after she turned twenty-nine years old. She worked at the mill for nineteen years, until it closed.

*Marjorie Terreault at a perch, 1955*

Marjorie started working days in the upstairs mending room. She and others mended holes in the unfinished cloth. Some of the older women who had worked there for years were not very helpful, and Marjorie thought they might have been worried about losing their jobs. "They didn't want to give anybody else a chance," she said.

Menders brought bolts of cloth, with seventy-five to one

hundred yards on each bolt, down over rollers. Against a light they could pick out the burrs with burling irons. She showed me a burling iron she still has in her sewing drawer. It looked like a pair of tweezers. She also showed me a burling needle. She said, "On unfinished cloth it wasn't very difficult, but weaving in the yarn on finished cloth just right, so that nothing showed, was very tedious."

One morning when Marjorie first started her job, she was afraid she was going to be late for work, so she was rushing. She took a pair of socks out of the drawer and threw them over her shoulder. But then when she was putting them on she could not find one, so she got another pair. When she arrived at work everyone started laughing. "The sock was still on my shoulder!" she said, laughing heartily.

When it was discovered that Marjorie had previously done office work, she was offered and accepted a job in the main office. "In my department, we had big ledgers with columns to fill in, and we had to keep track of every piece of cloth that came in and went out of the mill. When it got shipped out, we had big tickets with all the information of the cloth on them.

"The tickets were filed in a big drawer. Every week we had to give a report and we had to make sure that everything was in those books right to the 'T.' If a customer was inquiring about material that his company had ordered, you had to know everything about it. Customers were other mills that were going to make clothing out of the material." I was surprised to learn that Calvin Klein was one of Stevens' largest customers!

Marjorie told me the following story and emphasized that it was not funny. "Every fall we had to take inventory of the cloth at night. The cloth was stored downstairs in the basement in the wet finish room. We had to read everything on the bolts and write it down. All of a sudden this big river rat ran by us! Boy, I tell you, we climbed those rolls of cloth so fast to get away from that rat! We were scared to death!"

Marjorie remembered that she and Stella Bonk were the last two women to leave the building when the mill shut down. "I can tell you the exact date, December 15, 1970." At the end, she worked at the switchboard, because Pauline Bergeron was starting another job. It was necessary to have someone at the switchboard while the mill was being cleaned out.

Marjorie said, "Stevens was a nice place to work and they were good people." In the office they always had birthday parties and someone would make a cake. She often did too, and once as a joke, she made a cake using a large sponge. She decorated it with frosting, delighting everyone. "Bill Fisher, the office manager, was a wonderful person for joking and having a good time and a wonderful person to work for.

*Stevens Mill Float, Franklin Winter Carnival, 1966*

"Foster Blue, the superintendent, was another one. We had to count the shipping tickets and record everything that left the mill. We had a little tin typewriter table, and he'd come up behind us and slam his hand on the table, and we'd jump so high! I used to swear at him a little bit, because I was frightened, and he got such a bang out of it!"

*Stevens Float, Franklin Winter Carnival, 1963. Photo taken in lower back yard near boiler room; Lorraine Rudd riding in front.*

Marjorie was totally involved with all the activities of the mill and loved every minute of it. She bowled on the company bowling team, and worked diligently on the Stevens Mill float for the Franklin Winter Carnival.

She enjoyed the Christmas party every year. After the party, she invited friends and colleagues back to her house for still more food and partying. She would bake a ham and make pies. She hid numbers on several chairs and plates, and then gave prizes to those who sat on the chairs, or got the plates. She made sure she showed me the lovely casserole gift dishes that she chose one year from the Christmas catalogue that Stevens used for gift giving.

One year Marjorie won first prize for her costume at a Stevens Mill summer outing held annually at Bear Brook State Park. She made the costume using all Stevens Mill material. Her prize was two Revere Ware hot plates. She hurried to the kitchen to get them to show me.

As I looked around Marjorie's home, I could see one of her hobbies was collecting dolls. They are beautiful and sit and stand almost like real-life people everywhere in the house. Many of them are the well-known Annalee dolls.

She also was in the process of crocheting a blanket for a baby gift the day I was there. Around the room were table scarfs she has embroidered and cross stitched. And she still tries new recipes! I felt blessed to meet this delightful, energetic, and still very busy lady.

*Marjorie Terreault, 1956. Stevens Mill outing at Bear Brook State Park. Marjorie won First Prize making costume out of Stevens fabric.*

*Stevens Mill Complex, undated; courtesy Paul Gagnon*

*Postcard, Stevens Mill, Franklin, New Hampshire, undated*

*Franklin Stevens Mill, early 1900s—author's uncle, Stephen LaPlante, third from right; courtesy Franklin Historical Society*

*Franklin Stevens Mill, early 1900s; courtesy Franklin Historical Society*

*Franklin Stevens Mill, early 1900s—author's uncle, Stephen LaPlante, fifth from right; courtesy Franklin Historical Society*

*First row: Louis Gadrow, Marion Campana, Bob Dinan, Dot Adams, Crawford Dickinson.*
*Second row: Fred Durham, Maurice Limoge, Roger Desrosiers, Roland Desrosiers.*
*Third row: Reggie LaPlante, Bill Kelly, George Sargent; 1951, courtesy George Sargent*

*First row: Armand Marchand, Bert Welch, Mickey Brassard, Raymond Roy, Reggie Kent, Bill Fisher, Guy Haines; Second row: George Sargent, unknown, Archie Innis, Emil Bonk, Ray Spofford, Vern Shaw, Alan Milnes, Fred (last name unknown).*
*Undated; courtesy George Sargent*

# James Keniston

I arrived at the Keniston farm in East Andover, New Hampshire to meet with Jim, on a beautiful late summer day. Lovely shrubs and flowers were everywhere. My mother's paternal grandparents lived in this house at one time, and I remember visiting a great-aunt there many years ago.

Jim, who is a distant cousin, was born on April 27, 1921, "just up the hill from where I live now," he said. His birthplace once belonged to relatives of my mother's maternal grandfather. Except for three years in the United States Army Air Force, he has always lived in East Andover.

He and his wife, Dorothy, have four children. Dorothy joined us during the interview and contributed to the conversation as we talked about Jim's years at Stevens Mill.

He worked the day shift at the Franklin mill for eighteen years, beginning in 1952, and ending in 1970. Along with his day job, Jim also raised heifers on the farm. Dorothy said they were able to manage and take care of the farm "by working hard, nights and weekends."

Jim's first ten years at the mill were spent wrapping the cloth, one bundle at a time, in kraft paper before the cloth was sent to shipping. The paper was pulled from a roll and wrapped around the cloth, then taped at the ends. The wrapped rolls were dropped into a cart and taken to the shipping room. He and another man wrapped forty to fifty rolls an hour. From the shipping room, the cloth was sold to companies that made it into clothing. Later, he worked in perching where he inspected the cloth for defects.

Jim said working in the mill was not too bad considering he spent a lot of time there making a living. Dorothy thought he would spend the rest of his life working there. For Jim, the mill closing was the "best thing" that happened to him, as he found another job with better pay and a better retirement plan. But for some others, especially those who were middle-aged, it was unexpected and quite a shock.

After the mill closed, Dorothy said many of the men who had worked there spent a lot of time standing, talking, and visiting with one another on Central Street, Franklin's main street. Dorothy saw them when she went shopping, and said it was as if some of them had aged ten years in a few months. "You could see the anxiety in their faces."

Jim could not think of anything he did not like about working in the mill. Dorothy said they formed a lot of friendships. "A lot of it was a family thing." If they met people from the mill, they would stop and talk, and their children knew many of the people, too.

Working at the mill was also convenient for the family since it was a short commute. They did all their shopping in Franklin and all the services they used were there, which made bill paying easy. The children attended Franklin High School and often were able to ride home with their father.

Jim said he did not have time for hobbies when he was working. "My hobby was taking care of the cattle and working on the farm."

In spite of their hard work, in later years Jim and Dorothy have enjoyed quite a bit of traveling. They have traveled cross-country to visit their son in Oregon, where he works in forestry. Some of their other destinations have been Dollywood and Florida.

# Helen Minard

My interview with Helen Minard took me to the Peabody Home in Franklin, where I met a most gracious lady eager to answer all of my questions. She was worried, however, that she had nothing of interest to tell me. I assured her that everyone has a story to tell.

Helen was born in 1913. She began working at Sulloway Hosiery Mill in Franklin when she was just sixteen years old, and said she spent most of her life there. Sometime after it closed, she began working at Stevens Mill in Tilton on the second shift, 3 P.M. to 11 P.M. "I enjoyed it, because I could sleep in the morning. That was my downfall," she said, laughing. She worked there from 1960 to 1970. Her husband, now deceased, worked as a weaver in both the Franklin mill and the Tilton mill.

Helen worked in the weave room feeding full bobbins into the weavers' looms. Her job, as well as the women who worked with her, was to fill magazines with yarn-filled bobbins. A magazine was a container on the end of the loom. As the loom went back and forth, the bobbins dropped in automatically. When the bobbins ran out of yarn, they dropped into a bucket. "The men and women weavers tended to their looms. We were on one side and they were on the other," she said.

She further described her job. "We were required to run ten or twelve looms depending on what the work was. Of course the heavier the yarn, the harder you worked, because the yarn ran out quicker. We had these little bobbins—about eight to ten inches long—that were made in another department. They went into shuttles and that brought the filling (horizontal threads) into the cloth."

Helen did that day after day, after day, and I questioned whether she got tired of the work. "No, see Sulloway folded up and I stayed home a year and it was so good to get back into mill work!" She said she enjoyed working in the mill and she considered the people she worked with her friends, even though they did not really do anything or go anywhere together outside of work. "You know, you spent at least eight hours with them, seven days a week, sometimes. You worked so much, you didn't have that much time to socialize by the time you came home and took care of your other duties." She said she worked forty hours a week unless they had a rush job or something special, and then they worked seven days a week, even Sundays. They received extra pay for any overtime.

Helen said there was not much time for visiting or gossiping on the job. "It was so noisy in the weave room you had to get up to a person's ear and communicate that way. The only time was when you got caught up in your work, you'd sit on one of the benches and talk, but not for long!" Helen's hearing did not seem to be affected at all, in fact, I was surprised at how well she could hear. However, she said the noise in the weave room affected many people's hearing.

She did not feel they were overly watched by their bosses. "You had your assignment and you did it. They knew you were busy and they knew you weren't getting into any trouble," she said. "Depending what kind of job we were working on, we ate our lunch on the run. Sometimes if you had a real busy, busy job, you were allowed fifteen minutes and someone replaced you, and then you could eat your lunch, but mostly it was on the run."

There was a designated smoking area and if it was a hot night they could go outdoors. It got very hot—hot from the machinery and hot from the weather. A fine mist coming down from sprinklers onto the material also made it humid. "Sometimes, we'd feel the mist on us. It came in spurts."

Even though they did not have much time for chatting, I asked if they were aware of others having fun. I told Helen it seemed like they did not have as much fun as the men seemed to have. She said, "It was mostly the fixers who had time. The machine would be going and if it broke, they'd fix it. In their spare time they'd probably have time to fool around. Men are more social. The women had their noses to the ground. But the men, too, were busy tending to the looms; there were twelve to oversee."

Helen had only praise for the mill. "I was glad to have a job. The job was a safe job. They had everything in tip-top shape. Everything ran smoothly."

I asked if she had any interesting stories to tell me and she said, "No, it was all work." We chatted for a while as I hoped for perhaps something more. But she only reiterated, "The job was all work and no play. Do you know what I mean? I overheard a girl at the mall one time say she would put in her time for five dollars an hour. I never made five dollars an hour!"

When I asked if she had any hobbies, Helen answered, "Not really. By the time you worked and did your housework, you didn't have spare time. I would generally go outdoors and rake the leaves or tend to the lawn, or something like that. I did like to be outdoors!" She told me she did not have time for walks either.

Now, she enjoys her television, but "not those silly afternoon shows!" She likes *Good Morning America* with Diane Sawyer and Charlie Gibson, because they seem "so natural." She also likes *60 Minutes*. After all her years of working, I told Helen she surely deserves to enjoy her television.

# Ruth Walt*

Ruth Walt, also a resident of the Peabody Home, is Helen Minard's sister-in-law. Ruth did not know I was coming, but she invited me into her room with a smile. She, too, was sure she had nothing of interest to tell me, but was happy to talk with me.

Ruth was born on October 13, 1904. During her working days, she worked at both Sulloway Mill and the Needle Shop, alternating between the two. In 1954, she started working at Stevens Mill in Tilton and worked there for fifteen years. She began with the third shift, then second and finally first. She liked the first shift best, because she received a lot of overtime.

I asked Ruth to tell me about her job. "There isn't much to tell except we worked to keep the weavers going. I filled magazines with yarn-filled bobbins, just like Helen did."

Ruth said the job was not dangerous, but you could get hit by a shuttle "if it came out flying." It wasn't something they worried about, however, when they went to work. During the weaving process, if the weavers hit a snag, they had to break all the threads in the warp and the threads all had to be tied back in. Either the women did it, or if the weaver had time, he fixed it.

Ruth did the same thing every day until she neared the end of working in the mill. Then she became an inspector and inspected the quality of the yarn. "If it was a small area that was bad, you had to cut it above and below, realign it, and take out the bad." She received an hourly rate, but she could not remember how much she earned. "That was a while back, probably less than two dollars!."

Did she like working in the mill? Ruth replied, "It was a job." It appears it was a job for many of the women, whereas most men said they enjoyed working in the mill. Some of her co-workers were her friends, but working

---

* *Died June 4, 2001*

nights, she did not have much time for socializing. I mentioned that Helen had said it was hard to talk and visit on the job, because it was too noisy. Ruth agreed that being in the weave room was very noisy.

In the beginning, Ruth brought her own lunch to work. After a while though, the workers could buy lunch from machines. "You could put a nickel in for coffee or a sandwich, anything you wanted!" She really liked that and began to regularly buy her lunch.

I asked Ruth if she could remember anything humorous that happened in the mill but she could not think of a single thing. When I told her that some of the men had told me funny stories about things that had happened, and that I always knew men had more fun than women, she laughed and laughed. She commented there was not much time working on the magazines and it was heavy work. "You were a busy little girl!"

In her spare time, Ruth enjoyed crafts—knitting, embroidery and handwork. Some of her beautiful creations are framed and hang on the walls of her room, their bright colors immediately eye-catching.

She also used to knit sweaters for herself to wear dancing. "I was crazy about dancing," she said. Ballroom dancing was her favorite, and she went dancing often.

When I asked this pleasant lady, who looks years younger than her age, whether she had anything else to tell me, she replied with a twinkle in her eye, "No, it's all done and behind me."

# Ernest Gilman

"I was born right here on Bow Street and I'm still here on Bow Street," Ernest said. That was on Flag Day, June 14, 1927. Some twenty years later Flag Day again became an important day when he married his wife, June, on his birthday. He said, "I can never forget my anniversary—my anniversary, my birthday and Flag Day—all on the same day!"

Ernest enlisted in the navy in 1945 along with five or six other students while they were seniors in high school. They were told that if they enlisted before graduation they could still receive their diplomas. He said they had a party on a Monday night and had to report to Manchester Tuesday morning, so they did not get any sleep! He was a Seabee. Seabees were members of the construction battalions that built harbor facilities, airfields, etc. Ernest served for two years, and was stationed in Hawaii, in Japan, and in Guam. He worked with Japanese prisoners rebuilding homes and constructing new homes.

He began his eighteen years of working at Stevens Franklin Mill in the card room on the second shift in 1952. His boss was Phil Clark. "He was a fisherman and a hunter like I was, so we got along great," Ernest said. "I was the feeder on the back end of the card where the raw materials were put in. If you did not mind wool and you did not break out, it was not a bad job, but it was pretty hot in there on second shift." Reflecting further, he said, "It was a steady job and I always had work," echoing what was so important to almost all of the people I interviewed.

The mill was still making blankets for the army then and, because it was a government project, they had young men just out of college checking the process and inspecting the wool as it came off the card machine. Ernest said, "Phil had worked there for at least twenty years and got irritated with the young guys pulling a hunk of wool out of the machine in order to check it, and overseeing his work." Laughing, Ernest said, "Phil almost threw one of them out one day, because he was telling him how to run the card."

After a year in the card room, Ernest went to the Tilton mill as a spinner, where he also worked on the second shift. He said it was a neater job and he made more money. Spinning paid by the piece, plus a base rate. I asked if he minded working second shift and he said, "No, it was a good way to save money because you couldn't do anything else."

Timekeeping for spinning and weaving were separate jobs. Ernest said timekeepers set the clocks on each machine by the fastest workers. "You really had to move to keep up with them." At the end of each shift the clock was read to see how much material was put out.

He explained, "People who worked on the spinning frames ate when the machines allowed them to eat. Each spinner had three to four machines to keep running. There were six spools that had to be dropped into the frame. If you had good material and you put a spool in, it could last eight hours and you did not need to worry about it. With a bad job though the ends constantly needed to be retied." I mentioned that the women I had interviewed said spinning was a hard job for a woman. Ernest agreed that pushing the wagons around, loaded with the wooden bobbins, plus the material on them, was heavy work. Also, the wheels often got caught and tangled on the waste that had fallen onto the floor.

There was not much time for fun in the spinning room, but Ernest recounted a story from his first day at work. "Bill Kelly was the boss. After half a day of working, I asked Bill where the men's room was. Bill walked me out the door and pointed to where it was. But as I was walking down the ramp, I saw a man coming out of the bathroom on the opposite side. So I turned around and Bill was up there laughing. And this is the boss, on my very first day, so you see everyone got along!

"One thing I can say about Stevens Mill was they were not afraid to stockpile material even if it didn't sell for a year," Ernest said. "In shoe factories and like jobs, if the company stopped selling shoes, people were laid off, but J.P. Stevens never did that. They kept us going. Casket lining cloth—people are going to need that forever—pool table cloth, army blankets."

Ernest told me he made decorative hornets' nests out of bad yarn pulled off the bobbin, especially if it was grey yarn. He said the yarn was shaped just like a hornet's nest. Then he made little bumblebees out of pipe cleaners and attached them to the bottom of the nests using transparent fishing line. When he finished, he tied the nests to the ceiling. A fine mist, sprayed in the spinning room to keep the static down, caused the bees to constantly spin around. I could see that Ernest enjoyed his hornets' nests as much as I did the story.

Ernest liked working in the mill. He said, "We were all locals. We all knew each other. We worked together and we played together on weekends. We took turns going to different houses to play cards. We played bid whist, threw in a few pennies, and then in summer we'd take all the kids up to Wellington State Park at Newfound Lake."

Ernest's last seven years at the mill were on first shift as a loom fixer, working on two floors with Maurice Limoge. "It kept me busy!" he said. He liked the work and the job paid even more money. When the mill closed, Stevens gave their employees severance pay and maybe a little profit sharing—all in one check, Ernest remembered.

The drive between Franklin and Tilton was his answer as to whether he disliked anything about working in the mill. He drove east into the sun in the morning and into the sun again in the afternoon, heading west as he drove home. "That was terrible!" he said. I responded with, "It still is." We laughed at my little joke and he said, "That will never change." There is a lot of fog in that area and Ernest remembered the times he was not able to see the road. Often, his passenger, John Coffey, a fellow worker, rode with the door ajar, so he could guide Ernest along the yellow line.

Without a doubt, Ernest has been a very busy man. He participated in both Cub Scouts and Boy Scouts for twenty-seven years. He was scoutmaster for ten of those years, and in those ten years, he had ten scouts who made Eagle Scout. "It broke a record at that time," he said.

He also belonged to the Knights of Columbus and became a Grand Knight. He has been a member of the Elks Club for twenty-four years and is a life member of the VFW.

Ernest's hobbies are fishing, hunting, and golf. He plays golf at Den Brae in the Twilight League. He said, "I haven't shot a deer in twelve years, but I still go hunting, because I love to be in the woods." His wife said he likes the outdoors so much that she has threatened to move his bed outside. He also enjoys gardening, especially flowers, in his back yard. With his boundless energy, I can imagine they are beautiful!

# Lois Woods

I traveled to Franklin to interview Lois on an extremely windy, fall day. The home of Lois and Ernest Woods sits at the end of Lawndale Avenue in a large open space with several very tall trees that were really swaying in the wind.

Lois was born in Franklin on September 7, 1924. She said she had been away to attend Concord Commercial College and to Florida a few times with her sister, but that Franklin had always been her home.

She worked at Stevens Mill for seventeen years, beginning in 1953, when she was twenty-nine years old. She worked days in the shipping office as a teletype operator, typing orders and reports onto a machine, which sent them over telephone wires to the main office in New York City. In return, Lois received shipping information back over the teletype machine. No one else had mentioned this job and I expressed surprise. She said she was the only person who did that job, although another girl sometimes worked part-time with her. "The job was pretty interesting."

Lois liked working in the mill. She said, "No one was pushing you. You had your chores to do. A good group of people, too." There was nothing she did not like about working in the mill. "I never had a grumble or anything. It was a nice place to work."

Co-workers were her friends and everyone got along well. She said they gossiped but nothing bad. She did mention one girl who was there for a short time who just did not fit in. She did seances throughout the day. Laughing, Lois said, "You'd think she was in another world."

When the mill closed, she and another woman, Rachel Mercier, were the last two people to walk out of the building. "Even now it brings tears to my eyes." As she spoke, Lois did indeed have tears in her eyes. Clearly it had been an emotional time for her. Workers were asked to transfer to Georgia or the Carolinas to some of Stevens' southern plants to work, but she did not wish to.

Lois related that people who worked for fifteen years at the mill received a retirement. When she found out about it she was thrilled. "It was a big deal!" In fact, she had just cashed her monthly retirement check for $15.83 the morning of my interview. Her husband used to say it paid for the water bill. But Lois exclaimed, "It doesn't even do that anymore!"

Lois and Ernest work together tending to their flowers and a large vegetable garden. While taking care of the garden and their large property consumes much of their time, Lois says they derive much pleasure from it.

# Sheldon Morrill

I met Sheldon at the edge of his garden on a beautiful spring day in April. He told me gardening was one of his pleasures. Dressed in a tattered, navy blue sweat shirt, he looked like the perfect gardener to me.

As we walked to the house, he pointed to the road and said that he was born in Franklin, "right up the road here on Lawndale," on April 30, 1927. He has always lived in Franklin and graduated from Franklin High School in 1945. He and five other seniors graduated early in order to join the navy during World War II. He served for four years. Graduating early from high school to join the service during the war was a common occurrence. Sheldon and his wife, Olive, have four children.

He began working at Stevens Franklin Mill in 1951 when he was twenty-four years old. He worked for nineteen years, from 1951 to 1970, and then stayed another year to help close the mill. He worked in the power plant the whole time he was at the mill. He said, "When I first went to work, I was a boiler operator, which was shift work. We fired the boilers with coal. It was backbreaking work, but I didn't mind working!"

Coal was brought by train in coal cars and dumped at the trestle across the street from where Sanel Auto Parts Company now is on Central Street. From there it was brought by truck (in earlier years, oxen and carts were used) to Bow Street where the steam plant and boiler plant were located. Large and small chunks of coal were dumped into the crusher. From there, the conveyer took the coal up to a big hopper at the top of the plant, over the boiler room. Gravity brought the coal down movable chutes into the stokers.

Sheldon said, "In the old days there were four stokers. The stoker dropped into an auger. Reciprocating pulsating steam stokers pushed the coal in, but the coal overflowed the grates where it was supposed to burn. The hard part was that all the clinkers would fall on the ash and had to be pulled out."

When I asked if the clinkers had to be pulled out by hand, he answered, "Oh yes, with big long eight foot hoes and bars. I could hardly pick one up when I got there. I was a small person anyway. So, a couple guys like George Bean—he had been there a long time, an old Franklin resident—he helped me out. I did that for maybe four or five years.

"It was dirty work. No matter how you washed, you always had your eye shadow. You breathed a lot of coal dust, too. There was coal all over the place. When the coal came down the chutes, you'd have spills on the floor to shovel up. It was hot work!" About the time that Sheldon progressed to the engine room from the boiler room, the mill purchased an oil burner.

He stated, "The engine room was a one story structure with a couple of cubicles in it, and the heat really settled in there. We had three steam engines. One was an old engine, a Corliss, that had a horizontal engine and it took up about eighty feet with a thirty-six inch wide belt on it."

The engine room work force consisted of an engineer and an operating engineer. Bob Dunstable was in charge of the plant for a period of time. Later, Sheldon was put in charge of the power plant. "That's the one that burned in the recent fire, burned flat!" he said. "You could see the steam engines projecting up above the rubbish. The boiler room was on the west end of the brick concrete structure, and the engine room was easterly of that, and further easterly was the brick building that's still standing."

Sheldon explained his job in the engine room to me. "It was like being a mechanic. We were in charge of the power production. The mill was sustained on its own power most of the time. Only during periods of low water flow did we have to purchase power.

"We produced about ninety-five to ninety-nine per cent of the power, plus we had water wheels. The water helped supplement the power. We had two hydros (hydropower plants), one on each side of the river. All the generators were hooked into a grid and whatever power we didn't get from the water wheels had to be made up with the steam engines. The steam engines

*Top—upper dam; bottom—steam and water pipes crossing the river; 1969*

provided the necessary amount of electricity that was required in lieu of the water."

Sheldon said mills were built by rivers to utilize water power. "We had a pretty sophisticated water treatment system. Stevens used 2,000 to 2,500 gallons of water a minute, most of it heated. The water from the river was purified in a large concrete basin on the Bow Street side of the mill. It then flowed by gravity, due to the height of the dam, to the sand filters. All the solids and impurities were filtered out, as the water passed through the sand. After the water was taken out of the river, it was pumped back across the river to the finishing part of the mill.

"The finishing department of the mill used a tremendous amount of hot water to wash the cloth, so to make it economical, the engine room utilized all the exhaust steam. The heat from the steam that was driving the engines went through condensers and hot water heaters, to heat the water to process the cloth."

Sheldon remarked that it was noisy in the engine room. "It was not as noisy as some parts of the mill, but when the turbines were whining, oh yeah, the pumps and things like that, especially the steam engines, oh yeah, it was noisy, but it wasn't unbearable."

He did not think the power plant was a dangerous place to work. "There was chlorine and stuff, but we weren't as excited about it back in those days as they are now. I had chlorine leaks in an area, and we could smell it, but instead of calling the National Guard or the Fire Department we took care of it ourselves! They put on this big thing about asbestos after the fire. There were tons of it in there. That's what all this big up-to-do was about, removing the asbestos. The big pipes were all covered. The boilers were all covered. I've probably eaten a lot of it, because I worked there for twenty years, then I went down to Concord Steam and worked another eighteen to twenty years, but I don't know, I'm still here."

When Sheldon had X-rays of his lungs before heart surgery, Dr. Mishcom could see the fibers in his lungs, but Sheldon does not think it ever bothered him. "It's just like everything else in life, you may be one out of a thousand it might bother. No, what I did with all that asbestos didn't bother me."

He recalled some pipe fitters came in one day. They were throwing the asbestos around and heaving it at each other. "It never bothered us. I'm from the old school like my father used to be." Laughing, he said, "There's been a lot of changes in the last seventy years."

When the mill closed, Sheldon was in charge of the boiler room, the engine room, and the water filters. When I asked him if he liked his job, he answered, "Yes, I guess so. I like work anyway! If anybody ever asked me about working at Stevens—you talk about family—it was one great big family! No adversity with the people. Different people in there, but everybody seemed to get along with everybody else's personality." Sheldon said that even though he was a boss, there really was no bossing. Everyone worked for him. "We had to work hard. That's the way it was! It was a great place to work."

He added, "At that time Stevens was a pretty attractive place to work. They paid better wages than Sulloway Mill or the Needle Shop or the Hacksaw Shop. That's all there was in Franklin in those days. I worked at Sulloway's summers when I was going to school, but Stevens was the place to work! If you came from a family who worked there, you kept getting new jobs."

Sheldon said he was not the type of person who told jokes or played tricks on other people. "I was not that much of a trickster. I just paid attention to business. We had a lot to do and we couldn't fool around with the type of work we had to do."

As several other people had mentioned, Sheldon said they always had safety meetings once a month with the supervisors and a representative from each department. "Sooner or later, everybody ended up serving on the safety committee." The overseers or the State came from time to time to show slides on safety—even about automobile safety before vacations in the summer.

*Group of men at a safety meeting, 1969*

I asked Sheldon if there was anything he did not like about working in the mill. "Oh, I don't know. No, I don't think so. I didn't mind working nights, I guess, because I had plenty to do during the day. I either had other odd jobs during the day working for a contractor part-time, and this or that or whatever, to help supplement our income. You know, it wasn't the highest paid place, but it was the highest in Franklin."

Sheldon's wife, Olive, said he has always been involved in the community. He served on the Franklin City Council for six years. In fact, he was named Citizen of the Year for 1999. When his children were young, he did scouting and was a cub master. He also worked with Little League.

He was associated with the Franklin ski area when he was at Stevens. They needed help machining some parts on the tow one time, Sheldon said. "The mill was really receptive to community stuff. That's how I got involved. I'm still there! I do a lot down at the church. I'm one of the trustees. We keep busy on projects. I used to do a lot of fishing, but you work out of it." I laughed and said I always thought fishing was something you worked into when you retired, and that made him laugh.

It was easy to tell from talking with Sheldon that he has always been a hard-working man and still is very busy. "I like it that way!" he says.

# Edmund Nowak*

"We had a boss at Stevens who always told us, 'When you leave here, you're going to find a difference.' At the time you don't believe it, but I found out it was true," Ed said. "Stevens trusted their workers."

Ed was born in Franklin on January 26, 1923, and grew up there. He said that until recently he had lived on Bow Street almost all of his life. He and his wife, Marion, have two living children. They lost a son when he was a young adult.

Ed served in the army on two different occasions. He said it was a funny thing because each time it was for only a year. The first time was from 1948 to 1949. Then he served again in the Korean War from 1950 until 1951 and traveled as far as Japan.

He started working at Sulloway Mill in Franklin, and when it closed in 1953, he went to Stevens Mill where he remained until that, too, closed. He worked in the dye house department, but he did not actually participate in the dyeing process.

He described his work. "When the cloth came in, it was eighty-five yards long. My job was to sew the ends together to make it a complete piece. After the cloth was dyed, it went on a folding machine that squeezed the water out of it like an old-fashioned wringer washing machine." From there he took the cloth to the dryer. Ed said they had to wear low boots to keep

---

* *Died July 25, 2000*

their feet dry. "Because of the boots I was tagged with the nickname, 'Boots,' which stuck with me."

Ed said a lot of tiny fibers called "flock" came off the cloth and that each department was responsible for cleaning up its own area. I asked if he felt the fibers affected his health, but he said he did not think so. He thought probably those who worked with the dye might have been affected.

I shared how I had been told about the men taking a bath in the dye kettles on Saturday nights. Ed laughed and said that by the time he worked at Stevens they had showers, but that he had taken baths that way at Sulloway Mill. He explained that was because at home most people in those years had to heat water on the stove and put it in a washtub in the middle of the kitchen floor. "So, the big kettles made for a better bath."

Ed continued, "Stevens Mill was a good place to work. We had a lot of fun. They didn't push you and it was more friendly than the next job I had. If you wanted to sit down, you sat down. The company was so good that sometimes I think people took advantage of it. Everyone got along well too." Then he added, "But of course there were always one or two that were hard to get along with."

He liked the company bowling team and said they had good banquets at the end of the season. Ed belonged to the Polish American Club, as did many of his fellow workers in Franklin.

Over the years, he enjoyed softball and watching sports on TV. He also liked to attend the high school sporting events.

A tall man with a ready smile, Ed seemed to be a man happy with the way his life has gone.

# Raymond Gaudette

*Raymond Gaudett holding picture of M. T. Stevens Company First Annual Outing, September 6, 1941*

"When I was a teenager during World War II, I took my father's hot dinner to Stevens Mill at noontime," Ray said. "I also carried dinners for several of the neighbors. A child carrying a hot dinner to his father and, even to his neighbors, was a common practice at that time." Ray was paid ten cents a day for each lunch that he carried.

Laughing, he said, "On really cold days, instead of walking along Smith Street to get to the mill, I would walk in the front door of J. J. Newberry's Store and out the back door to the mill gate, carrying four or five lunch pails." I thought what he was doing must have been very obvious, but he said no one ever stopped him.

There was a barbed wire fence around the millyard Ray told me, and a watchman at the gate so that no Germans (during World War II) could get into the plant. One cold day, the watchman (Ray called him The Caboose) was not there, so Ray lifted the fence, crawled under, and went into the building. He delivered his dinners and when he came out the watchman stopped him saying, "Boy, how did you get in here?" Ray said the watchman was so mad! Ray thought it was pretty foolish that they put up a fence so no one could get in and bomb the place, but that if he could get in, he thought it would be pretty easy for the enemy to get in too!

Ray was born on March 8, 1931 in the house he still lives in. He married his wife, Lucille, in 1953, and they have five children. He worked at the Sulloway Mill in Franklin for many years and when it closed he got a job at Stevens Mill.

He worked at Stevens for a little over seventeen years. He began on the third shift, but had difficulty sleeping during the day, so he told his boss he was going to quit if he could not work second shift. His boss moved him to second shift and later to first.

Ray's first job was picking up bobbins from the spinning room, and putting them in the steamer. Before long he became a spinner, which he did for the rest of the time he was at the mill. Ray said, "Spinning keeps you busy!"

The spinners were spinning wool, and later, rabbit hair and mohair.

A fine mist came from sprinklers to keep the dust and static down, so workers were not allowed to open the windows. Yet, dust and fibers flew around anyway. To keep their machines clean, spinners used a hose to blow the dust out, but Ray said the only thing it did was blow the dust all over the place.

"One day the 'big boys' came in when I was blowing, and the dust blew all over them! I didn't know they were there!", he chuckled. He said that many of the workers who have died, died of cancer. Because of the mist from the sprinklers, it was very damp and cold, especially in winter. Ray thought that was the reason he had pneumonia one year.

He remembered that in the early days, workers were paid in cash on payday. Someone went to the bank and brought back the payroll in a large envelope.

Everyone got along well, but laughing, he said, that he got "ugly" once in a while. Like the others he enjoyed the mill sports: basketball, softball, bowling. On weekends he and his wife often enjoyed playing cards with other mill couples.

Ray is a member of the Polish Club. He also likes hunting, regular fishing and ice fishing, as well as gardening. He enjoys participating in activities with his children and helping them with their projects. Recently, he remarked that for the very first time in his life, he had helped one of them put on a roof!

# Theresa Parenteau

At her home in Franklin, Theresa assured me she had nothing to share, even though she had conscientiously taken the time to write down a few things about her life and the twenty-one years she had worked at Stevens Mill.

Immediately, Theresa told me she could not recall anything she did not like about working in the mill. She said, "Especially in our age we knew we had to work, and when you had a job you did the best you knew how. And it felt good to earn money."

Theresa was born in St. Isidore, Quebec, about twenty miles southeast of Montreal in 1927, and she grew up in Canada. Her father died when the children were quite young, and they went to live at a convent which served as an orphanage. She came to the States in 1948 when she was twenty-one years old to care for her aunt's children, Madeleine and Theresa, so that their parents, Joseph and Marie, could work.

In 1949, Theresa began working second shift in the weave room at the Franklin mill. When they moved the weaving to Tilton in 1950, she went there to work and worked days. She said she was lucky that she had agreed to go. "Some people didn't believe they were going to move some of the work to the Tilton mill, so they lost their jobs. They thought they were going to stay put!"

Her job began with "dropping wires." On a big frame in the weave room she had to separate each thread and drop a long rounded wire with a space in between to hold the thread in place. Workers had to go from one loom to another. She said the work was constant with no real time to rest.

Theresa also filled magazines with bobbins of thread. Another job she did was draw the ends into the fabric before it went on the looms. She performed the same jobs in both Franklin and Tilton. She proudly said, "I used to be a good teacher. I taught people to fill the magazines and drop wires. One time I had three young girls at the same time. It was so noisy in the weave room that I had to shout as I taught them."

Near the end of my interview, I said there was a question I always asked. And before I could ask it, she said, "You want to know if I liked it?" Then she replied, "I did. I did!" She said other workers were her friends and they celebrated Christmas and birthdays together and went out to eat. "Everyone felt bad when the mill closed."

Theresa was on the mill bowling league during her working years. "I was not a great bowler, but I had fun," she said.

Theresa belongs to Catholic Daughters. She and her husband, Robert, have one daughter who lives in Colorado. Visiting her there has allowed Theresa to see a different part of the country. Over the years she and her husband have enjoyed their return trips to Canada to visit relatives.

# Raymond Hersey

"At forty dollars a week, if you didn't get overtime, you didn't have much spending money. Overtime made the job worthwhile!" Ray remarked of his years working in Stevens Mill.

Ray grew up on a farm in East Andover, New Hampshire. He was born in 1921, the youngest living child of my maternal grandparents, Guy and Nannie Hersey. Ray is my uncle, my mother's youngest brother. A veteran of World War II, Ray was awarded the Purple Heart for injuries he received during combat in the Philippines. He and his wife, Dorothy, have three daughters. They recently lost their only son.

Ray worked at the Franklin mill from 1953 to 1961. He worked the second shift, 4 P.M. to 12 P.M., for quite some time, and then finally the day shift. He folded out the cloth in the grey room, which he said was the front end of the job process when the cloth came from the Tilton mill to be finished at the Franklin mill.

Ray described his job for me. "The cloth came on eight or ten rolls. You put a rod through the roll and it went into the folder. After the cloth was folded out, it was put in a truck and pushed downstairs to go to different operations. Some went first to the carbonizer and some went to the washers or fulling mills." After working on the folders, Ray's next job was getting things out of storage. He had a list every day of so many rolls of "this and that" that was needed for the three people running the folders. "I graduated from the folders to bringing in and supplying the folders!" I asked him if he got a raise. He told me he did not, but he found running the folders got to be pretty monotonous. "You had to keep bookkeeping there, how many yards were in each roll and the number on each ticket." He was happy to have a change.

Men who brought things in from storage had to go to different areas and buildings to get what was on the list. The cloth, wound on big cardboard spools, was about four feet wide. Some of the spools had a lot of yards on them, while others did not have many. The spools were separated by brands into different piles in open-ended boxes, and they found what they needed out of the boxes.

Ray spent his last three years at the mill on the platform crew. First thing in the morning, the crew picked up all the rubbish and took it to the dump. Then he said, "There'd probably be a forty foot truck back there at the mill to unload, sometimes with soap or detergents, and we'd put everything where it was supposed to go. Also, every day there would be a load of cloth from the Tilton mill to put in the storage building on Bow Street. That's the one that burned in 1998."

There were four "fellas" on the crew and they worked in two teams of two. I asked Ray if it was heavy work and with a look of exasperation, he said, "Sometimes the cloth would come in and there might be three trailer loads with four guys to unload it, segregate it, and put it into storage!"

In addition to his other duties, during his last three years on the job, Ray drove a two ton, company truck, plowing snow and sanding the driveways, "so people could get into the place without breaking their necks." He still took things to the dump. Ray said this job was more interesting, more diverse, but still the same pay.

When Ray first applied for a job at Stevens, a guy (he called the men either a guy or a fella) took him down to see what he would be doing and showed him "all these bobbins that he'd pick up off the machines." Ray was rather skeptical about the job and asked, "You must have to pick those up more than once, don't you?" And the guy answered, "Oh no, just one time a shift." There were twenty-eight of them. Ray replied, "Well, I'm going to be pretty busy I think! Then I found out there were four more machines around the corner and they never did tell me about those." I asked him if the bobbins were big and he said, "Big enough!"

In spite of his skepticism about the work, he told the man, "Well, I'll try it." Since Ray had told me earlier that he had started working on the folding machine, I'm not sure when he performed this job. He continued telling me what the job involved. "There were metal trucks that you threw all this stuff in. Then there was another truck to put the empty ones in, then you had to weigh all that stuff and put it down on a piece of paper, the brand, and this and that."

"Oh, another bookkeeping job," I said. He replied, "Yeah, I mean, you couldn't be a dumb cluck. If you couldn't read or write, why you couldn't do that stuff! I could see why some of those guys wandering around doing nothing, why they didn't want to do that kind of a job. They watch you!" I remarked, "You had an immediate boss then?" Ray answered, "Yeah, but he's dead now just like all the rest of them."

Because some of the alleys were too small to get a truck through, he had to go downstairs and get an arm load of the bobbins, come up and dump them, take the empties, and then go and get another arm load. Part of the time was taken up with the "bookkeeping" while the machines continued to run. "Twenty-eight bobbins," he said, "would have been great, but with thirty-two, it never ended and you were getting behind. It lasted all night long and you never could catch up."

I asked Ray if he remembered any accidents. He said there was one bad one and that it was amazing the guy lived. Some men were working on machines trying to tighten up something when someone threw a switch. "A long attached wrench rapped the guy on the side of the head. He was lucky to be alive."

Dot, who was reading in the next room, reminded Ray of his own accident which he claimed was a "lot about nothing!" He explained that in the mending room, there was an elevator with a cable. When the cable was pulled down, the elevator came up.

One day a man was moving some wet, heavy cloth and he could not push it, so he wanted Ray to help him move it onto the elevator. Just as Ray was about three quarters of the way on the elevator, someone pulled the cable and it started to go down. The man had not locked it, so Ray reached in to pull it the other way to get it back up again when the man jumped on! Just as he did, the gate came down and grazed the top of Ray's head. He said, "It bled like a stuck hog, running off the top of my nose, and it looked a hundred times worse than it was!"

He told me that of course he still had hair then and showed me the top of his bald head and said there was probably a scar still there. But try as I could, I could not see one.

He was taken to the office and the nurse was sent for. Ray wasn't sure why she became a nurse, because she couldn't stand the sight of blood. "So then they got the boss's secretary to sop it up," he said. She told him he had to go to the doctor, and summoned someone to take him, while Ray all the while protested he did not need one.

Finally, the doctor came in and asked what the problem was. Ray said, "Hey, I don't have to be here, all it did was graze my head and tore the skin and made it bleed in great style." The doctor looked at his head and said, "All that damn fuss over a little scratch like that." Ray shot back, "Hey, it wasn't my idea, believe me, it's their idea, they're afraid they're gonna get sued, and all this and that! The doctor didn't even put tape on it and remarked that everyone made a 'mountain out of a molehill.'"

I inquired whether Ray liked working at the mill or if it was just a job. He said, "Oh, it was all right. I mean it wasn't that bad and it was one of the few places you could make a living." When he knew I was coming to interview him, he searched his dresser drawers for his W-2 forms. He had them for years he said, but must have thrown them away. Ray said, "One good thing was the chance to work overtime. Most people who worked in the mill were just glad to have a job and they were sure of their jobs. They weren't getting rich, but they were making a living."

He could not really remember anyone telling jokes, but he thought that they probably did. "There are always some guys who like telling jokes." Even if he could recall one or two jokes, he laughingly told me that I probably could not use them.

He remembered that Marilyn Monroe died when he was working in the mill. "That was a big topic around the mill when that happened. Nobody could believe it! Everyone was saying, 'Well, did you hear that on the radio?' Of course not everyone had television then."

I asked Ray if he enjoyed the men he worked with and were they his friends? He said, "Yes, they were more civilized than they are nowadays." I laughed and agreed that was probably true and he responded, "That's the truth. Most everybody got along. There's some that, you know, did a lot of fooling and somebody played a trick on somebody else." I asked if he could remember any and he said, "No, it was too long ago and most of my life in the mill I tried to wash out of my mind anyway!"

As we were finishing our interview, Dot joined us. I told her I was interested in what she liked or disliked as a wife of someone who worked in the mill. She responded, "One hard thing was being home alone at night because the children were young." She liked that the pay was steady, and that they had health insurance, which many places did not have. She also liked being able to buy cloth at the mill. It was twenty-five cents a yard for beautiful wool and she made lots of clothes for the children, even a coat for herself.

Ray and Dot have traveled extensively and have been to all but five states of the continental United States. They are also big country music fans and have attended many shows in Nashville, Bronson, and Hershey.

I have enjoyed listening to Ray's descriptions of people and events over the years. In spite of his many travels, it is clear that his speech and mannerisms have not traveled far from his native New Hampshire roots.

# Virginia Dufault

I interviewed Virginia on a misty, fall morning in September at her home on Webster Lake, where she has an apartment in her daughter and son-in-law's house. The beautifully well-maintained yard was filled with gorgeous flowers. Immediately, I felt at ease as Virginia welcomed me and told me to take a chair. She looked elegant, as if she had just stepped out of a fashion magazine.

Virginia was born in Brighton, Massachusetts on February 5, 1916. She frequently visited her grandparents who had a summer place on Webster Lake in Franklin. When she was eight years old, her family moved to Franklin, where she has lived ever since.

She started working at Stevens Mill in Franklin when she was forty-seven years old, and worked there for seven years, until the mill closed. She was a styler on the day shift, 7 A.M. to 4 P.M. She registered all finished products of the day.

Virginia's job required filling out forms and recording by number, where the material was, the condition it was in, and the different phases it had gone through. She then sent the reports to the office, and that particular bolt of cloth would be ready for shipping.

At the time that she started at Stevens, inspection workers were working overtime until 9 P.M., Virginia said. "They would have a stack of work piled up ahead of me which kind of floored me in a way." That was because the man who "broke her in" said there was nothing to the job. He told her if she could get three hundred pieces a day she would be doing well, and to always walk around the mill with a pad of paper and a pencil and act important! "So I figured this is a snap. Before I got through, I had to 'holler uncle' and they had to get someone to help me, because when they were working overtime, I was doing two days work in a day. I hated to give in and say I couldn't do it". She said she found out there was more to the job than just walking around and acting important. "The fellow who broke me in on the job, that's what he would do, walk around and act important, so he could work overtime. But women weren't given overtime!"

Just before the mill closed, the company built a new office and she was in it with about fifteen to twenty other workers. She remembered that Bob Dorman and Rita Keegan worked in the office. Before work, Virginia said she and Connie Cheney would go into a little rest area to see who could finish a crossword puzzle first before starting work.

I asked if the workers joked or teased one another in her area. Laughing heartily, she said that when they were in the big office Ted Campana's desk was a few desks away from hers, and with paper clips and a rubber band she could make his life miserable. "We used to have some fun," she said. It was like a big family and she felt her co-workers were her friends.

She also laughed as she told me about Jim Magoon responding to a fire. He was a call fireman for the city of Franklin. There were metal spiral stairs between the different floors. Jim worked on the top floor. The office where Virginia worked was one floor below. "When the city fire bell rang, what a racket! Jim would go down those stairs like he was shot out of a gun and he never missed a fire."

Virginia especially enjoyed working at the mill because she had worked for a dry cleaning business doing counter work previously, and working at Stevens was more of a sitting-down job. She stressed that no one really had time to socialize outside of the workplace, but she remembered that once, just the "girls" went to the Margate Inn in Laconia. There was live music and they danced with different gentlemen who were there. "It was good!" she said.

Company Christmas parties were held at the historic 1893 Opera House, better known now as Franklin City Hall. She said they had some wild times, but good times! As mentioned by so many other workers, she recalled the company picnics held at Bear Brook State Park and Gunstock.

Not one to shirk her civic duty, Virginia served two terms on the city council. She also spent many evenings for thirteen to fourteen years as a member of the school board, where I'm sure she made her presence known!

As I was leaving, the smell of apple pie wafted from the kitchen where her son-in-law was baking. She said he is a good cook and that she is fortunate to have a nice place to live.

# Wayne Cilley

I arrived at Wayne's home in Franklin on a beautiful, but almost unbearable, hot day in June. The weather had been very dry, and he was watering his lawn. He welcomed me with a big smile.

Wayne was born in Franklin in 1935, where he has been a lifelong resident. He was in the National Guard for six years and took a tour of duty for six months in a regular army program. He and his wife, Margaret, have five children.

His fifteen years at the Franklin mill spanned 1955 to 1970. He went to the mill soon after high school. He said there were ten children in his family and people did not think of college as a choice the way they do today.

When Wayne first became employed at the mill, he worked in wet finish on the third shift: napping, gigging and cropping. "In wet finish," he said, "material that had to be sponged, in other words ready for the needle, was sent out to American London, a sponging house in New York. Sponged meant preshrunk with steam, so that the material did not shrink when it was washed. There were routines with every set."

Sending material to American London to be sponged was very expensive as they charged by the yard. So the company decided to do the process right at Stevens with the help of Arthur Swenson, the chief adjuster for the J.P. Stevens Company. That way the finished goods could be sent directly to the customer. Wayne said, "That wicked expense was eliminated."

Soon after he started working, the mill had a big layoff and most of the help was gone, including him. "They only kept the oldest hands," he said.

When Wayne was called back to work a short time later, he worked in the winding room on the first shift. "You can't get winding confused with winding where they weave cloth," he said. "They have winders there too, but it's altogether different.

"The winding job consisted of getting pieces of material that were examined, putting each one on a tube, rolling it up and cutting out the bad parts (the remnants). Then writing the yardage down on the piece tickets that came with each individual piece. The finished yards were obtained by deducting the remnants from the piece. From there it was put on a conveyor belt and weighed. I did that job also," Wayne said.

He also retrieved items for the rest of the help. Tubes were stored across the river. "We had to walk over with a hand truck, fill the truck, and bring it back over. We kept the flat boards over there too, for double fold winding. We put the material on a machine and double folded it like you would buy it in a remnant store."

After a couple of years on that job, Wayne went into the examining area, which was a step previous to winding. He said it was a better job with more pay. People with a little more seniority were asked to work there, because the job required a little more responsibility.

Wayne said examining the cloth was done mostly "with the eyes." Examiners were called perchers. "There were at least a dozen big picture windows on the north side of the sixth floor to get just the right light to see the colors. Perchers had to make sure there were no streaks, manufacturing problems, yarn pulling problems, holes, etc. At the time, there were eight men and eight women working in the examining room. The women used power perchers—machines which had a lever they could push—to make the fabric drop down in front of them. After they examined it, the fabric folded out into a truck. The men had to move the cloth by hand. Eventually, in the early 1960s, power perchers were installed for the men, too."

There were specifications for perching that were set up by Arthur Swenson. He knew all the people in the retail business. He came every now and then, and pieces of cloth that were of questionable quality were kept for him to examine to see if he could sell them. "Mr. Swenson came up with the fact that you could have just so many defects in a piece of cloth. Generally, it was eight defects per cut. Every now and then a new edict allowed a couple more defects. There could be one defect per ten yards, so that ten, instead of eight defects, gave a little more leeway, rather than having A, B, and C seconds."

Wayne said, "The job was a job where you had to keep on your toes. You had to shade the pieces out, piece to piece, end to end, and across the piece to see if it was level." I asked whether the job ever became boring and Wayne answered, "It never was for me!"

As examiners, Wayne said, "Probably lots of people didn't like us, but we had to be particular examining the cloth, because if we had a lot of seconds we wouldn't be making much money. We used to harp and scream and holler and things like that. It was final inspection!"

When the examiners finished the process, the material went to the winding room in a truck, then to the weighers and out to a wrapping table. Next, the material was put in boxes, placed on the elevator, and taken down to the shipping room.

Before the pieces went down in the elevator they were all styled by hand which meant placing the style number, the book number, the color number, and the piece number—everything that was done to the cloth during the day—onto the material. "Virginia Dufault did that job, as did Ronnie Adams for a while. I got to know a lot of people," Wayne said.

When the mill was really busy, the workers worked from 7 A.M. to 9 P.M. Their regular hours were 7 A.M. to 4 P.M., with an hour off for lunch. If they worked until 9 P.M., they got a twenty minute to a half hour break before starting work again.

Wayne continued, "When J.P. Stevens decided to make the Franklin plant their finishing plant, it was big! It included the Tilton mill, which always had over one hundred looms. We had Worumbo material, one of the big styles that J.P. Stevens acquired when they bought out the Worumbo Plant in Lisbon Falls, Maine. We also had several plants in Massachusetts: Marland Mills, Osgood Mill and J.P. Stevens Plant in Andover. Stevens also bought out Forstmann Woolen which was a noted textile firm. We got all their griege goods, also considered 'white goods,' because they were just woven, as well as a lot of material dyed as plaids. Charlie Pierce and Joe Adamczyk were brought up to work in the finishing room. Stevens was smart in that respect. When they bought a place out, they also brought some people to the plant with knowledge about the processes.

"Before the mills combined and Stevens received all the weaving for finishing, we did 1,600 to 2,000 pieces of work a week. Afterwards, we did 2,500 to over 3,000 pieces per week. That meant more jobs were created, as well as more overtime. Summer help was needed then with many recruited from the local high school.

"One thing a lot of people didn't like to do was pass on information. That was a big thing at J.P. Stevens. The older hands did not want to tell anybody anything!" Wayne said that was an old idea. They were afraid they would lose their jobs. However, Wayne said he was never like that. If he learned something, he passed it on. He said, "Knowledge is the greatest thing!"

For Wayne, working in the mill was a good experience. He said all the people were good to work with and he met a lot of people along the way. He responded with a big "Oh yes, definitely," when I asked him if his co-workers were his friends. He did a lot of fishing with many of them, including deep sea fishing, ice fishing and smelting. One of the superintendents, John Foster Blue, sometimes joined them.

Many of the workers enjoyed weekly card games together. "We played poker for money. All the people who worked there got along so good. Nobody got mad, it was just fun!" Wayne said. "Back then a few bucks meant more. Today you get a few bucks and you wonder what you're going to do with it. The wives made up something to eat and we'd have tea or coffee. Some workers had a quarter pool with about thirty to thirty-five people. You threw a quarter in—that's when a quarter was a quarter!"

Wayne remarked that he was very serious on the job, but remembered going by the coffee shop to pick up donuts for the whole crew from time to time. He also recalled a couple of men bringing great, big jars of pickled eggs to work. It was kind of a joke. Everyone wondered how they could eat "those things." Wayne said he was younger at the time, and the men were ten or fifteen years older. They were used to eating "things like that!" But he learned to enjoy them too!

While working at Stevens was a good experience, Wayne said the company was backward as far as wages and insurances were concerned. "We all felt the same. We liked the place; we liked the people, but we worked long hours. We didn't realize it until we went somewhere else.

"The company did come in finally with a little profit sharing plan that benefited everybody. We were vested in ten years which is outdated now. But it was a start in the right direction. The hourly wages were horrible. Stevens was never known to pay very well. It was a known fact! Working a lot of overtime is how I got this place (his house).

"Speaking of overtime, taking trips to Bear Brook State Park came in during L.B. Johnson's Great Society," Wayne said. "It was the period we worked so much overtime. Things were getting better because the Franklin and Tilton mills combined operations, and the Franklin mill was doing all the finishing.

"In the late fifties or early sixties, workers tried to get a union. But management, mainly Alan Milnes, who was the superintendent and a very nice man, said that if they did, the company would move, because they were totally against unions. This scared some of the people. Well, it didn't matter; they left anyway, didn't they?"

Wayne told me that later on he worked in two other firms, but none could duplicate Stevens women's wear. "We had a turbo treat machine (a high speed machine) in the wet finish with heating elements across the machine. It put a mirrorlike finish on the cloth."

Wayne belonged to the J.P. Stevens bowling team, and he and his wife belonged to a square dancing club for five years. He wanted his five children to go to college, so they would not have to work in the mill. He told them, "It's all right to work in the mill, but if you don't have to.... People worked hard. I know these people; they worked a lot of hours. They didn't take trips and they didn't have much family time."

Wayne was very conscientious while we were talking. He wanted to make sure I understood everything he was talking about and that I got it right. He laughed when I told him it sounded like he must have been a valued employee. Of that I have little doubt!

# Thomas Beattie

"I was treated very well at Stevens Mill. They gave me the opportunities I wanted and I never had one complaint." As the boss in the Stevens Mill sponging room, Tom said he had beautiful cooperation from maintenance. He could ask for something to be done and it would be done. "I was taught things from the maintenance crew that I didn't know, and that was important to me."

Tom was born in Franklin on May 3, 1922. The family soon moved to Meredith Center. His mother died in childbirth with his younger brother when Tom was three and a half years old, "a very traumatic time," he said. He spent six and a half years in an orphanage in Manchester and then more time in foster care.

In 1940, when Tom was eighteen years old, he joined the National Guard and was soon called to active duty in Texas. He spent some time in Australia, a place he loved. From there, he served in New Guinea, the Dutch East Indies, and the Philippine Islands, as well as completing other duties. While serving, he was wounded and spent six months in the hospital. He was overseas for forty-one months before returning to Franklin. Later, he served in the Korean War, this time for a year and a half in the air force.

Tom has been married to his wife, June, for fifty-three years. They have a son and a daughter. June joined us for the interview and told me that she had worked at the mill for a very short time before Tom did, while he was in Korea.

Tom spent fourteen years working on the third shift at Stevens Mill. He began as a shear hand in 1953 when he was thirty-one years old. After four years, he was named a supervisor in the sponging department. The company had tried pre-shrinking its cloth, a process called sponging, but the technique was not very successful. Those in charge believed it might be less expensive to send the cloth out to some other plant for sponging, but then they decided to try the process again.

Tom's responsibilities included managing two machines, an open sponger and a double roll sponger. He made some successful changes and modifications to some of the machines so they could do sponging in-house. He said, "The company made damn good money on it."

There was no night boss on duty, so Tom said that he had to rely on the responsibility of his personnel on the second and third shifts. "They would get a little rambunctious sometimes, but we managed." He thinks he only had one argument in ten years and that his men enjoyed having him as a supervisor. "We understood one another and my men and I got along and worked together."

He told me about the exhaust system that was used in his area. "We used steam with everything, and there were hoods over the machines. We had this monstrous fan that would change the air in the big room four times in one minute. Those fans were so strong! Many mornings there would be pigeons in the room, and a lot of guys would go in and purposely start the exhaust system, and blow the pigeons out into the river." Tom said he did not like that, but that he could not be on the men all of the time.

Perhaps to soften the story, he added that another time they "chased down" a bird. "I got to work and my men were running up and down the room. We exhausted the bird and I got hold of it, held it, and let it go out the window."

Tom stressed that he had his principles and was fussy about the quality of his work, refusing to work on cloth that was not good. He liked his boss and they got along well, but sometimes his boss wanted him to sign a paper on goods that Tom thought were unsatisfactory. He told his boss that if he thought the goods were satisfactory, he could sign them himself.

"Absolutely," Tom answered when I asked him if his co-workers were also friends. In fact, he could not praise everyone enough. "I think I had the best crew of men that any boss could ever want!" When I originally called Tom to ask if I could interview him about his years of working in Stevens Mill, he told me he would be glad to "cooperate" with me. Cooperation must be one of the finest words in the dictionary, and I suspect, the reason Tom and his men got along so well.

He is a life member of the Elks, as well as the Disabled American Veterans. He also belongs to the VFW. Along the way he worked in Cub Scouts and with the Franklin Drum Corps. He said he really enjoyed the Drum Corps and he took kids all over Maine, New Hampshire, and Vermont for competitions. His hobbies have included hunting, fishing, and sports over the years.

Tom turned to his wife with a smile when I asked him if he had had a good life after a rather difficult childhood. She returned his smile and he answered, "My life has been a good life!"

# James Horman

"I was born into it. Working in the mills was a natural thing to do, because both of my parents were weavers in a mill. "When I met Jim he had already written down some notes about his days at Stevens Mill so that he would be prepared for me. Several people had suggested I interview him and told me what a nice man he is. I was not disappointed.

Jim grew up in Dracut, Massachusetts, where he was born in June 1919. He attended Lowell Textile, which is now the University of Massachusetts at Lowell. He said he began his years of working in the mills right in his hometown at the American Woolen Mill.

With his wife, Catherine, and their six children, he moved to the Franklin-Tilton area in 1960, from North Andover, Massachusetts, where he had been working at Stevens North Andover plant. He was transferred to the Stevens Tilton-Northfield Mill and promoted to assistant superintendent. Later, he was made superintendent and remained with the mill until it closed. Jim worked for the J.P. Stevens Company for a total of twenty-six years. He seemed pleased that he still has the last shuttle from the Tilton mill.

As superintendent, Jim was responsible for the overall production at the mill. Part of his job required traveling to the Franklin plant every day from Tilton to see how everything was operating in finishing. "I'd just stop in and see how everything was going. Cloth to be finished went to Franklin from Tilton on a roll that was folded back and forth on trucks, and then put on a trailer. There might be twenty to twenty-five pieces on one truck."

He explained the terms for the dying process in different plants. "The Stevens North Andover, Massachussets plant was known as a stock dye plant, which meant the wool was dyed before it was made into yarn. The Tilton plant was a piece dye plant. They made the yarn natural. Then the cloth was dyed at the Franklin plant. The mill in Dracut, where I started with J.P. Stevens back in 1946, was also a piece dye plant."

Jim added and expanded on some of the information about the manufacture of cloth that I had already obtained from others. For instance, in the picking process, where an emulsion was put on the wool, Jim said, "People say you can't mix oil and water, but we did it every day of the week - with Borax! That's the secret."

Like others, he reiterated the dangers of working in the card room because of the rolls and the thousands of wires sticking up, and the possibility of getting something caught. Jim reluctantly told me what he said was "a sad story" about one of the workers. "A real young fellow got his sleeve caught on the wires. His arm was dragged right into one of the rolls and he lost his arm." Jim was impressed that within three months the young man was back at work with an artificial arm and able to use it.

"In the spinning process, the yarn was twisted and drafted (pulled) to get the size yarn you wanted. The emulsion process allowed you to do that. After the yarn was spun, it went into a steam box (a container) to condition it for about a half hour. Otherwise it would just spin around and be difficult to handle. From there it went to a cone winder where the yarn was wound on cones, some small and some large, then put onto spools.

"After the spooling, there were enough spools to make a warp that was put on a big beam prior to weaving. After it was made into the warp, it was taken to the weave room. The weave room put harnesses on it, then drew the yarn through heddles. A heddle is about twelve inches high with an eye in it (like a needle).

"After the harnesses were drawn in, we had many girls just drawing-in, prior to putting the warp yarn in the loom and weaving. We also had a knot tier. When one warp was all used, we saved enough yarn to tie on to another one, and then just pulled it through the harnesses. After the warp was made and the harnesses put on, it was placed into the loom. The loom was started up and the shuttle went back and forth to weave the cloth."

Jim loved working in the mill. "The mill was the only industry in the town where I started, so naturally everybody flocked there, a lot like Franklin in its early days."

Because he was the superintendent and the boss, I asked if he thought people were afraid of him. He laughed, and said "Of course not." I told him that must mean he was a good boss.

Every Christmas a gift of ten dollars was given to each person on the payroll. Jim personally went to every shift to give out the money. One man was just starting his very first shift at 12 midnight. Jim called him in as he was going by his office and handed him a ten dollar bill. Surprised, the young man said, "A ten dollar bill! What's that for?"

"It's a Christmas bonus."

"But I haven't worked five minutes."

"Your name is on the payroll, so you're entitled to it."

Jim said, "He was tickled to death."

I could tell Jim was proud of his company as he told me of its many community involvements. One was the Winter Carnival. "We were always involved in the winter carnival. We sponsored a queen candidate." He said his daughter was a queen candidate in 1965 and his two youngest children rode with her in the parade on the mill-decorated float.

The Franklin Hospital had a lawn party every year to raise money. The mill always had a remnant booth at the party with all the proceeds going to the hospital. When the hospital was expanding, Stevens in Tilton donated thirty thousand dollars.

In 1963, when the company was 150 years old, a celebration was held with a big party at Franklin High School. "All the officials from New York came, including Robert T. Stevens, who was chairman of the board," Jim said. "At one time, he was Secretary of the Army under Dwight D. Eisenhower. During the Joseph McCarthy hearings, Bob Stevens was McCarthy's nemesis."

For many summers the Tilton plant hired a high school senior to work in the office. The company also took fourth and fifth graders through the plant on tours. "They were fascinated," Jim said. The children always wrote a thank you letter to him. Laughing, he said, "They'd write, 'Dear Mr. Holman'—they called it Holman—and everything else!" He still has the letters. He said some of them are "out of this world." I could tell Jim likes children.

He also mentioned the softball team and the bowling league. When he was forty, he was quite impressed when he first saw Bill Fisher playing softball at age fifty-three! I told Jim when he got to be fifty-three, he probably still played softball, too. He laughed and said he had just gone ice skating the previous weekend at age eighty!

Jim sadly told me his wife had died in 1994, but he said he keeps busy. He is involved in many civic organizations. Among them are: The American Legion, VFW, Third and Fourth Degree of the Knights of Columbus, and the Franklin Historical Society.

In the summer, he enjoys playing golf, which he says he absolutely loves, and he plays four to five times a week. In winter, he weaves scarfs, shawls, and rugs to give away. He also sells them at craft fairs. He showed me two of his scarfs and they were beautiful.

When I left, Jim told me he was going to a meeting of the VFW that night. He is truly a busy man with many interests.

# Barbara and John Cooper

"It was very rare that anyone got laid off at Stevens Mill," John said. "Instead, workers were cut to four days a week when necessary. Other times, rather than get a raise, pay was cut. Even when a raise was given, it was only two or three cents an hour. Those were the days when people expected to work for the same company for their entire lives, and the company did whatever they had to do to keep them."

Barbara and John met while working at Stevens Mill in Tilton. As frame spinners, Barbara said she and John did piecework. They had to tie in spools and piece the ends in a certain way. "It was very tricky. When the bobbins were filled, a new set had to be put on."

Their machines were next to each other. She said that was nice because they could help each other piecing and doffing. "That made it faster." Laughing, John said, "And then they brought in more machines for us to work on."

Barbara was born in 1932 and grew up in Northfield, New Hampshire, while John was born in Newfoundland in 1926. He came to Boston alone in 1947. He said, "A second cousin got me into the States and I worked for him for a while."

John served in the army during the Korean War. "I was one of the lucky ones. I went to Germany instead of the other way." He and Barbara have one daughter.

Barbara worked at the mill for nineteen years, beginning in 1952 when she was nineteen. John started in 1953, also in Tilton, and worked for eighteen years.

Stevens had bought Gibson's Woolen Mill and then added on to the building. When she started working, Barbara said, "The spinning room was all new and I think possibly the card room. There were three shifts around the clock and we ate our lunch on the run with no breaks at all." John said, "You always ate in a hurry, if at all."

In the beginning, Barbara worked the night shift—midnight to 8 A.M.—and she hated it! After two or three years she worked days. John worked third shift, then second shift, and then first. Barbara said working your way from third shift to first was a new rule the company had made after she started working.

Barbara and John received a base salary and then so much for the piecework. I suggested their pay must have varied from week to week depending on how fast they worked, but Barbara said it was pretty consistent. I suppose one can work only so fast!

John said it was more difficult to work on heavy material than fine. Some of the yarn was as thick as rope, so a spool ran out faster and spools had to be changed frequently. The spools with the nubby, heavy material might only last a half hour, but spools with fine yarn might go ten or fifteen hours. "In winter, we were making yarn for spring and summer cloth, and in summer, we were making yarn for fall and winter cloth. It was very hot working on that heavy material in summer!

"The job was hard, but except for a pinched finger or a bobbin that was hard to remove, it was not dangerous and we weren't a bunch of sissies like some today. It was all part of the day," John said. Barbara added, "People knew what a day's work was."

When I asked if they had enjoyed working at the mill, Barbara looked at John, who said, "It was a place to work, really. There weren't that many manufacturing jobs back then, so Stevens controlled the whole thing!" Barbara said they met a lot of nice people, many who enjoyed a good time. "Some of the setup men liked to play around by putting grease on the handles of their machines so they could not shut them off. Things like that." Both of them enjoyed the Christmas and summer parties.

John remarked that the thing he probably disliked most about working in the mill was the hours. He worked a lot of overtime and both of them worked a lot of Saturdays. They felt they had to work overtime to make ends meet.

In 1970, when John knew the mill was going to close, he had a chance to build houses with Barbara's brother. Because he didn't want to lose any of his benefits by leaving too early, he went to Mr. Horman, the superintendent, and told him about the job offer. Mr. Horman said, "You mean you have a job already?" Then he told John that if he had a job, to go ahead and take it and everything would be all right.

Barbara said Mr. Horman was a very nice man and knew everyone by name. "He could go through every room, say good morning, and address each person. I couldn't figure out how he knew our names so quickly. Even today he always speaks."

Examples of Barbara and John's many talents are evident throughout their home. Barbara likes to cross-stitch. The day I visited she was wearing an attractive sweat shirt with cross-stitching she had made. She said she has made so many shirts over the years that she has lost track of them. She has sold a few, but has given most of them away. Her beautiful framed cross-stitchings hang on the walls.

John has a woodworking shop in the basement where he does crafts and makes clocks, picture frames, and cabinets. Two solid cherry grandfather clocks stand in his living room. They are magnificent. The clocks are for each of his two granddaughters. I told him how very lucky they are to have such a clever and talented grandfather.

It is evident that these two, who met at the mill where they worked side by side, are still working side by side all these many years later.

# Colin Chapman

"I always worked the night shift while I worked at Stevens Mill. I preferred it, because I could go fishing afterwards, and then go home and sleep. I worked 7 P.M. to 7 A.M. It was a good life if you could handle it," Colin said.

When I arrived at his home, Colin was mowing the lawn, something he does a lot during the summer. He is manager of LaBranche Trailer Park in West Franklin where he mows many lawns, among other things. He lives there with his wife, Beverly.

He grew up in Laconia where he was born on September 11, 1934. During the Korean War, he joined the air force and served for four years, three of them oversees. He had duty in France and Germany, and visited other countries while in Europe. "It was an excellent experience," he said. "I saw a lot I wouldn't have seen otherwise."

Colin began working at the Franklin mill eight years before it closed, and worked the same job the whole eight years. He was a fulling mill operator in the wet finish department where they shrank the cloth. "The fulling mill was the first operation in finishing."

He told me about his job. "First, the cloth was soaped up. Next, it was put into washing machines, like huge washers. The water was very hot! The machines were set for so many minutes and then the cloth was taken out and measured to see how much it had shrunk. If it had not shrunk enough, it was placed in the machine again for a period of time and rechecked. From there, the cloth went into a heat machine, like a train on a track, to dry it out. Then it went upstairs onto a stretcher, and on to the dry finish department."

I asked if the soap bothered him, but he said they wore large rubber gloves that came to the elbow. They also wore boots, because the floor was very wet and slick when stretching the wet cloth.

Colin and his partner had to keep a chart with the amount of material and the minutes the cloth spent in the machines. "The superintendent might come by and you could be reading the paper, but you had to make sure you were keeping track of everything." He said the machines were very noisy and they had to get right in someone's face to talk.

Almost every night without fail, as he and his partner were eating lunch or reading the paper while their machines were running, two or three big rats would run by the machines. "The rats were big as house cats!" he said.

Colin also recalled how Mickey Brassard used to go to the Cape to pick up material. "Whenever he went, he brought back pickled squid for all the guys, and we loved it!"

When I asked him if there was anything he didn't like about working in the mill, he answered, "No, the way I looked at it, someone had to do it."

Colin is a life member of the VFW, as well as the Military Order of the Cooties (a fund group of the VFW). He also belongs to the Policeman's Association, the Elks, and the American Legion. He calls Bingo for the VFW on Monday nights, for the Soldiers Home on Tuesday nights, and for the Elks on Thursday nights. As if that's not enough, he calls Bingo at the Senior Center, too. He said he really enjoys calling!

He used to like fishing, but hasn't fished since 1978. He also liked to play golf. But now his hobbies are "mowing lawns and working."

When I left, Colin was preparing to do more lawn mowing. I told him that he certainly is a very busy man. He agreed and added that he also takes care of an estate in Sanbornton. A busy man, indeed!

# Jesse Carroll

I was greeted by Jesse and his wife, Rachael, on their front lawn. It was a beautiful, spring afternoon, and they were accompanied by their little dog, Princess Taffy. With ribbons in her hair, she truly looked like a princess, and I soon observed that she is affectionately treated like one.

Jesse was born in 1926 in Wananish, North Carolina. He was the only person I interviewed who grew up in the South. He left North Carolina in 1948 for New York state where he worked for three years. While there he met Rachael, a native of Franklin.

Drafted into the army in 1951, Jesse served for two years. He was a medic and spent fourteen months in Panama. After he was discharged from the army in 1953, the couple moved to Franklin. He was twenty-seven years old and his first job was at Stevens Mill. He worked at the mill until it closed, "when they kicked me out," he said.

He began as a hand tacker on second shift with Raymond Ross as his boss. Tacking was done after the weaving to keep the material rolled together, as it went to the fulling mills to be shrunk. The material came off the machine folded in half, and the tacker stitched the two edges together with a loop stitch that could be removed later. Jesse said the material could be tacked two or three times for different operations. "When the mill made billiard cloth, it probably got tacked three times."

Later, he moved to the griege room so that he could be on the day shift.

There, he was a cloth carrier. As the cloth got folded out on the folder in different sets, he took it to the dry cleaner, carbonizer, or wherever it was going for its next procedure.

"And then," he said, "believe it or not, farther down the road, I went back to hand tacking, only this time on the day shift." He said it worked out pretty well, because he tacked all the wet work for the steamer in preparation for the dye house. He had to tack the bigger cloth for the fulling mill and at other times for a different process. He knew pretty much what had to be accomplished every day and worked until it was done.

Everyone kept their own area clean. If some of the big company bosses were coming, everything stopped in order to make sure everything was clean. "No work would be done, but it would be clean!" Jesse said, laughing.

One day some "bigwigs" were in the mill and the workers were told not to go to lunch while they were there. Two of the workers spoke French and after a while, as they could see lunch time passing by, one said to the other in French, "Don't these people ever eat?" One of the bosses understood French. He laughed and laughed and said, "That's a good idea." So everyone had lunch.

Jesse liked the mill because "everyone did their job." He never had time to get bored. If he got caught up on his work, he just helped someone else.

Rachael worked at the mill for a brief time just before it closed. She said she was one of the last to be hired and one of the first to be let go. She said they had some fun. "One day, Doug Piper put a little lizard in some cloth to frighten me, and of course, it did."

Jesse belonged to the American Legion and the Polish American Club. He bowled on the Stevens Mill bowling league.

When I asked Jesse if he has any hobbies, his wife said, "His hobby is working at WalMart." He is a greeter there, and he says he absolutely loves the job! Having been graciously greeted there myself by Jesse, I think probably everyone there loves him, too!

# Denise and Roger Day

"There were some weeks when I worked almost one hundred hours at Stevens," Roger said. "Seven days a week, thirteen and fourteen hours a day, if there were rush jobs to finish. I knew different jobs, so I might finish work in one department, and at the end of the shift go to work in another department. I almost lived there."

Roger was born in Franklin in 1938, but he grew up in Hill, New Hampshire. His grandfather owned most of the land where the present town of Hill is situated. His grandmother kept diaries and wrote about the time that the old Hill Village "was moving in all around her" to its new location. Roger said she liked company, so he did not think it bothered her.

He enlisted in the army in 1956, "right out of high school," and remained until 1959. Two and a half of those three years were spent in Germany. Denise was born in Franklin in 1942, and grew up there on Elkins Street. She and Roger have a son and a daughter.

Denise worked in the office at the Tilton mill doing payroll for the weave room and general office work from 1961 to 1964. She worked with Reggie LaPlante in the same office as Roger Desrochers, who lives across the street from her and Roger.

Part of her job took her from department to department to pick up tickets from the weavers' machines bearing information of what they were working on. She laughed as she said she put the information through what they called a computer. "Nothing like any computer today!" She also made up tickets of what the weavers would do next, the type of yarn they needed, etc. The orders came from the upper office where Jim Horman was superintendent. Denise said, "Jim was the kind of boss you could go to if something was upsetting you and he would straighten it out right away. He was such a nice man."

Roger began working second shift at the Franklin mill in 1959, in the dry finish and sponging room, both part of the same department with Mickey Brassard as overall boss, and Tom Beattie as boss of sponging. In dry finish, Roger worked mostly on the decater, "a machine that pressed the material, rolled it up, and compacted it." Later he moved to perching.

Still later, Roger was promoted to the office in production, known as the customer service department, "planning the week's work for the mill." Roger said, "I called and talked to salesmen in New York. I was also an expediter. Salesmen would call wondering where the stuff was and when they were going to get it. My job was to go to the different departments, find out where the material was located, and then be sure it got out to customers on time."

When the mill closed, he accompanied maintenance on many truck trips to the dump to burn old records. "Somebody had to do it," he said. I thought that sounded suspicious or secretive, but Roger said, "Oh, nothing serious about the records. Just day-to-day bookkeeping stuff that wouldn't be needed anymore." Yet, it was his responsibility, not maintenance, to make sure they were burned.

Laughing heartily, Denise said she and some of the girls used to hide in George Sargent's office when they did not have much to do, and they did not want to be found. "You had to walk through the whole mill to get there and it was quiet. After a while, people caught on as to where we were hiding."

She had never really drunk coffee before she went to the mill, because she didn't like it, and she had never smoked. But the very first day when the girls went on break for coffee, she was too embarrassed to say she did not drink coffee, so she did. Then, when they offered her a cigarette she took that, too. She continued to drink coffee, but she said that fortunately she did not like smoking and soon was not too embarrassed to say so.

Roger told me that he and some of the men played chess during breaks. "The person who sat across the desk from me, Colin Jones, the other expediter, was a chess buff." He and Roger left the board set up on a corner of their desks and played whenever they had free time. "Sometimes a game lasted for two or three days. Of course if the boss was around, we didn't play." Roger said after they started playing chess, several people started playing, and they had chess boards set up in different locations around the mill. "I taught my son how to play and now I can't beat him."

Everyone got along well at the mill, Roger said. "You had arguments, but when you're together for so many years you have to get along." Because Roger's hobbies are hunting and fishing, he enjoyed going deep sea fishing with some of the men who worked at the mill.

Like so many others, Denise and Roger enjoyed the Christmas parties and the mill activities that Stevens held for its employees. Roger was very involved with its float for the Franklin Winter Carnival parade and rode on it several times. Denise said that at the time she was in the Franklin Junior Women's Club, and the club was always in competition with Stevens Mill for the best float. Even though Stevens had a large body of people and more equipment, she proudly said that the Women's Club won a couple of times.

In addition to the Women's Club where she served as president, Denise also belonged to the Business and Professional Women's Club. At present, both she and Roger are very involved with the Franklin Targeteers, a rifle club. They are charter members. People go to practice and just to have fun. The club has a range on city property on River Street Extension near the waste storage plant. They share the range with the Franklin police who also practice there.

When she worked at the mill, Denise always thought she could probably do better, but when she thinks back on that time she thinks, "Oh, those were the days." Even though she only worked there a short time, she and two or three others still get together.

Roger said the whole time he was at the mill, he was always telling everybody he was looking for another job, but "I didn't look that hard." He took the postal exam and passed it just before the mill announced its closing, but he remained at the mill to help shut things down. After that, he worked at the post office for thirty-two years.

Denise still works part-time, three days a week at the Dress Barn at the Lakes Region Factory Stores in Tilton. She works at the Dress Barn in Florida, too, where they spend the winter.

Denise and Roger say they are enjoying their retirement and their life.

# Prescott Libby

Prescott was born in 1941 in Hill, New Hampshire, "in that brown house down the road," from where his yellow trailer home presently sits. He said he has always lived in the area.

He started working in the spinning room at the Franklin mill when he was just a young man. He said it was so long ago that he does not remember how old he was. Shortly thereafter, he began working at Stevens Tilton Mill on the second shift, and remained there until it closed.

In Tilton, Prescott continued to work in the spinning room and at the same time, on the steamer. The steamer shrank the yarn. It resembled a large oven, approximately four feet by five feet long. His job was to put four boxes of yarn into the steamer. He showed me with his hands how he had to lift the heavy door, and then pull it back down again to close it.

After fifteen to twenty minutes, he removed the boxes and put four more into the oven. "The outside of the steamer got really hot," he said, "so hot you couldn't put your hand on it." Some of the women I interviewed earlier told me they had warmed their lunches or drinks by putting the containers on top of the oven when they got to work.

Prescott said that while he waited for the yarn to steam, he did his work in the spinning room. Like so many others, he was so busy that he ate his lunch as he worked.

I asked if there was anything he especially liked about working in the mill and he said, "Not particularly." When I then asked if there was anything he did not like, again his response was "Not particularly." Later, he commented that he would rather have worked first shift.

Prescott said humorous things happened once in a while. One man made a dummy of the boss out of yarn with arms and legs and a "big fluffy head," and hung him up on a pipe. Everyone thought it was funny except the boss, but after a while he thought it was comical, too. A very serious man, Prescott could not refrain from smiling as he told me the story.

He has lived alone for a long time. He likes living alone and told me he never gets lonely. It may be the reason he is a man of few words!

# Tarnya Fredette

"It was so noisy in the weave room that there wasn't much talking or visiting," Tarnya said. "We used to communicate simple things by using sign language." She showed me how they signed for eating by opening her mouth and pointing to it, and for drinking, she raised her arm and tipped her hand.

Tarnya was born on Christmas Day, December 25, 1944. She has lived in Franklin most of her life. She married her husband, Ernest, in 1965 and they have one daughter.

She began working in the weave room at the Tilton mill in 1962 when she was eighteen years old. In 1965, when she wanted to get married, she asked for a week off. "The boss," she said, "told me the mill was short of help, and if I wanted to get married, I had to quit. So I quit." In late 1966, she went back to the mill and worked until it closed.

Most of the time she worked second shift, which she liked. She could go to the beach, do housework and other things during the day, and still have time to get to work by 4 P.M. Later, she worked days, but she said that was harder, because there were more bosses around!

Like Helen Minard and Ruth Walt, Tarnya worked in the weave room filling magazines. "No breaks," she said. "Put a sandwich in your pocket and take a bite, as you walk from machine to machine. It wasn't hard work, but it was a lot of standing and reaching. You'd fill your hands with bobbins and put them in the magazines. You'd have about fifty or sixty bobbins. If you didn't keep it filled, the whole machine would shut down and make a hole in the cloth." She said she learned to weave "just enough" from some of the weavers to be able to put a bobbin in the shuttle to keep it running if a weaver went on break.

I asked Tarnya if she felt a lot of pressure keeping the magazines filled. She replied that she did not think so. She and the other women developed a system. They would look around at the magazines and if they were all at the same level they knew they would all be empty at the same time. So they filled every other one, and then came back to fill the others. Sometimes, there were fifteen to twenty magazines to keep filled.

She worked in the small weave room most of the time, but because she was much younger than some of the other women, she was also responsible for six or seven machines across the hallway in another room. When she was filling those machines, she could not see the ones in the weave room. But the women helped one another. If one person's magazines were full and another person's were getting low, they helped fill them.

I inquired whether she had good relationships with the weavers knowing that if the machines stopped due to an empty magazine, the weavers would lose money. Tarnya responded, "Some of them were rather strange, but others would help us if they saw the magazine going down. Still others would get mad and yell and holler at us."

In July and August the windows were kept open in the weave room because of the extreme heat. She said it seemed to be hotter back then than it is today. The weave room was right near the river, and darning needle insects frequently flew through the open windows. "One night a green darning needle got onto the cloth. You could just see it spread out there! A large piece had to be cut out and it was sold at the remnant store as damaged goods. They didn't throw too much away!" she said. After that they were not allowed to open the windows and they "just had to sweat it out."

Another incident involved a snapping turtle that frequently climbed the river bank, crossed the parking lot, and went through an open door into the mill. Tarnya said, "When the turtle came in, it was like he was turning his head back and forth checking on the workers to see if they were doing their work. Men came from everywhere to take it out, as he snapped away."

Tarnya sometimes worked on the quiller. She explained, "The quiller was where the thread was put onto the bobbins. Big spools of thread came out of the spinning room to the quiller girls and we tied the thread into the bobbins."

The last year and a half that she worked at the mill, she dropped wires. She liked dropping wires. "It was fun putting all those little wires on the thread." She also did drawing-in. "The thread came off the loom and you drew it in through the harnesses to make the cloth."

Sometimes when Tarnya was filling magazines, men came up from the picker house covered from head to toe with wool fuzz from shaking the dirt out of the wool. If the job was dangerous to them, no one seemed to be too worried about it, she said. She certainly did not feel her job was dangerous. But, she realizes now that for some jobs workers should have worn masks, and in the weave room they should have worn ear plugs.

OSHA came into the mill during the last few years that she worked. She wondered if that was why the mill closed. OSHA demanded that they do certain things, for instance, allow workers to take breaks. "Of course we loved that!"

Tarnya enjoyed working in the mill and never thought about going elsewhere to work. She thinks everyone felt that way. Even when she worked overtime until midnight, went home, and returned at 2 A.M. for another two hours, she liked it. That was before she got married and she said, "It was something to do; I wasn't doing much anyway!" After she got married, she sometimes took over for someone and worked double shifts.

When I asked if there was anything she did not like about working in the mill, she did not think so. But then she said, "We always had more work than we could handle—but we handled it!"

I was fascinated by Tarnya's current business which involves reading tarot cards. She laughed and said, "My family calls me a witch." She has written a how-to course for others, which she monitors. "I wouldn't want someone to ruin a person's life by giving wrong information," she said.

She has read tarot cards for a long time, and thinks she was destined to become a reader of cards from when she was a young child growing up in Tilton, New Hampshire. She lived in a creaky, old, thirteen-room farmhouse with lots of attics. "We grew up with things going bump in the night. The old organ in the attic would play and other strange happenings occurred."

Tarnya asked if I had ever heard of Dionne Warwick and the psychic network, and I replied I had seen the commercials on TV for a number of years. Though she was never on TV, she said she worked for the psychic network up until the time it closed a few years ago.

I found Tarnya to be a very interesting lady. I really enjoyed meeting her and learning about her life in the mill, as well as her later years as a psychic. Fortunately for me, I felt only good vibes.

# Epilogue

These are just a few of the voices from behind the red-brick walls—proud men and women who worked hard at their jobs—because it was their job.

Intermingled with their mill stories, I especially appreciated learning of their resilience and about their philosophies of life. Without exception, the ideals of devotion to family, church, and community shone through in their lives.

Most of the people I interviewed still live in their own homes. This seems a testament that working in the mill did indeed provide the necessities of life, and more. When the mill closed in 1970, most workers went on to other jobs. It is clear, however, that the Stevens Mill years were not forgotten. As many said, "It was a life!"

*Stevens Mill main building, Franklin, New Hampshire, 2000*

# The Mill Today

On June 4, 2001, I toured the original J.P. Stevens main mill building in Franklin with Wayne Cilley, a former mill employee, and an interviewee in this book. The building is now called the Franklin Business Center. Over the mill years, the manufacturing and finishing, described in this book, took place in this 122,000 square-foot building.

The building has six floors with the basement being the first floor. Wayne said all six floors were basically open when the mill was in operation, with machines set up in different sections. There are still large open areas, but in many places partitions have been put up to accommodate office space, storage space, and small manufacturing firms, with long hallways to reach them.

Daniel Petrini is the present manager and owner of the mill complex. His office is located on the second floor as one enters at the main entrance. The Senior Center and several comfortable-looking offices also are on this floor.

As Wayne and I descended to the basement down the steep, winding metal stairs, Wayne said, "Oh, this is eerie!" The long, mostly empty, areas are indeed rather spooky. As we walked around the basement, we could hear the rushing water of the river against the north wall of the building.

While I thought we might see rats (remembering some of the workers' stories), we did not.

As we climbed the long flights of stairs to the different floors, Wayne commented that walking up and down the stairs was good training for everyone who worked in the mill.

From the parking lot, facing the main building, the long, low-slung dye house still stands. Wayne stated that this, too, was a long open-concept building, and a very busy place. In light of today's environmental concerns, Wayne said (almost as if not wanting to believe it), "All the effluent went into the river. The fish turned all different colors: blue, green, red." The building now appears to be used for storage.

While there is much activity throughout the old mill, it is hard to envision the days when hundreds of workers were busy throughout the three shifts and the family atmosphere that prevailed. Yet as we walked around, I could imagine the sounds of their machines and hear their voices. I know I am extremely fortunate to have learned little pieces of the lives of some of the people who worked there.

*Stevens Mill Dye House, 2001*

# A Brief Description of the Making of Cloth

Textile mills produced cloth, not clothing. The cloth was then sold to clothing manufacturers. Mill workers worked very hard tending the machines and resolving the problems.

The sheep's wool arrived at the mill in one piece called a fleece. Many pieces were delivered at once in large burlap bags. The wool was scoured to eliminate as many natural and acquired impurities as possible including dirt, wool fat, grass, sand, burrs, pollen, and other vegetable matter. Scouring machines consisted of tubs with inner bowls that had perforated sides to allow dirt to pass through. The wool was then dried.

Scouring did not always eliminate vegetable matter such as burrs and seeds, and so the wool also had to go through a process called carbonizing. The wool was placed in sulfuric acid, which caused the burrs to break up. The wool was then subjected to heat, converting the disintegrated material into carbon. The burrs were removed by crushing them and then shaking them out of the wool.

The picker machine broke the wool apart. Wool from several different lots were blended and mixed together to achieve uniformity in quality and color. Lubricants were also added to the wool to ensure good processing and to prevent static electricity.

From the picker, the wool was fed into carding machines consisting of large revolving rollers covered with fine wire teeth designed to separate the individual fibers and to line up all the fibers of wool in one direction. By passing wool across the rollers, the wool fibers were disentangled and emerged at the end as an untwisted rope called a sliver. Another procedure, combing, removed all but the long fibers and was an additional process if an especially fine thread was desired.

Spinning produced finished yarn. Before that step, the material passed through several other steps depending on the quality and type of yarn needed. Drawing stretched the sliver so that the fibers ran in parallel lines. Roving was a process that twisted and reduced the size of the fiber for spinning. The roving (the strand of drawn out fibers) was then placed on the spinning frame. Several strands were twisted together, depending on the finished product in a process known as twisting.

Drawing-in (not to be confused with drawing) was the last stage before weaving. Individual warp threads were drawn through eyes in the harness wires in a predetermined order. This procedure allowed the loom to weave the cloth in the appropriate pattern.

Weaving consisted of the warp (the yarn running the length of the cloth) and the weft or filling (yarn running perpendicular to the warp yarn) passing back and forth, and over and under the alternative warp yarn to produce cloth, by the action of the shuttle.

Inspecting the cloth, known as burling, followed the weaving process. Little knots or burls of wool were picked out of the cloth. If not removed, burls could cause the yarn to be pulled out of the material. Menders wove these threads back into the material by hand.

The unfinished cloth was then dyed. To make the colors fast, it was steamed and finally washed. Occasionally the raw stock (or yarn) was dyed before it was woven into cloth.

To remove the raised lint, the finishing department brushed, singed, and napped the cloth.

The cloth then went to the perching department for its final inspection. Lastly, it was measured, folded, and wrapped for shipment.

This process of making cloth has not changed much in over one hundred years.

Ronald Abear, who was vice-president of operations for L.W. Packard & Company in Ashland, New Hampshire for many years, listed each individual step for making cloth when I questioned him about how cloth is made today. The steps follow:

- Shipping and receiving of the raw stock
- Blending the wool with the picker
- Carding
- Spinning

- Rewinding
- Dressing
- Weaving
- Burling—grey room
- Carbonizing
- Tacking
- Fulling
- Washing
- Dye cycle
- Stretcher department
- Wet napper
- Wet shear
- Dryer
- Dry napper
- Dry shear
- Final finish—decater or sponging
- Perching—Final inspection
- Measured, wrapped and shipped

# Glossary

1. **Blending and Lubricating:** Wool from several different lots are blended together to achieve uniform quality and color. Lubricants are added to ensure good processing and to prevent static electricity buildup.

2. **Burl:** A wool trade term for an imperfection.

3. **Carbonizing:** A chemical process to eliminate vegetable matter such as burrs and seeds not washed out during the scouring process. The process involves treatment with an acid, as by the use of hydrochloric acid gas (dry process) or sulfuric acid solution (wet process) which causes the burrs to break up. Next, the wool is subjected to heat, which converts the disintegrated material into carbon.

4. **Carding:** Carding combs the clean dry wool to straighten the fibers. A carding machine consists of large revolving cylinders or rollers covered with fine wire or teeth. By passing wool across these cylinders the wool fibers are disentangled and emerge at the end in the form of a continuous web or sliver.

5. **Combing:** An additional step after carding to produce worsted yarn. The process arranges the fibers in a highly parallel form producing top quality yarns.

6. **Cone:** A conical support on which yarn is wound.

7. **Doff:** To take off or remove, for instance, to doff bobbins.

8. DRAWING: The drawing process serves to double the sliver, drawing it out to a thinner more uniform diameter that assures all the fibers are as parallel as possible.

9. DRAWING-IN: The last stage before weaving. The process where individual warp threads are drawn through the eyes in the harness wires in a certain order that allows the loom to weave a particular pattern.

10. END: An individual warp yarn.

11. FILLING: The threads running crosswise in a fabric. Also referred to as the weft.

12 FINISHING: The final step in wool processing is quality control inspection. A thorough examination of the cloth identifies imperfections which are removed or rewoven. Once this inspection is complete, the fabric undergoes a controlled shrinkage process called "fulling" to tighten the weave.

13. FLY: Loose fibers that fly out into the atmosphere during processing.

14. FULLING: A process in the finishing of woolen cloth. The cloth is dampened, beaten under heat which causes shrinking, increases the weight, and covers the weave of the cloth.

15. GABARDINE: A tightly woven, twilled, worsted fabric used for year-round business suiting.

16. GIGGING: The process of raising a nap on fabrics.

17. GILL BOX: A drafting machine, used in worsted processing, in which the motion of the fibers is in part controlled by pins fixed on moving bars (pinned fallers).

18. GRIEGE GOODS: A term used for fabrics before dyeing or finishing; also called grey goods.

19. HEDDLE: Like a large needle, about twelve inches long with eyelets at the top, which fits into a harness.

20. **Loom:** A machine used for weaving fabrics.

21. **Magazine:** An open container attached to the loom to hold filled bobbins.

22. **Napping:** A finish process that raised the fibers to the surface by means of revolving cylinders covered with metal points.

23. **Perch:** (1) A manually or mechanically operated device consisting of a system of rollers over which fabric is drawn at open width for the purpose of inspection; (2) To inspect fabric in a vertical (hanging) position or at an angle inclined upwards away from the source of light.

24. **Pick:** The pick is a single weft thread and interlaces the warp to form woven fabric.

25. **Piece Dyed:** Woolen goods dyed following the weaving process.

26. **Piece Goods:** Fabric sold by or from the piece (small bunches of wool staple taken during sorting and sold in lots).

27. **Piecework:** Work paid for at a fixed rate per piece of work done.

28. **Quilling:** To wind thread or yarn on a weaver's spindle or bobbin.

29. **Roving:** Relatively fine fibrous strands used in the later or final processes of preparation for spinning.

30. **Scouring:** The fleece is washed in big tubs to remove dirt, grease, and grass.

31. **Second hand:** Equivalent of a shift foreman.

32. **Shearing:** A sheep's wool is removed in one piece called a fleece.

33. **Singe:** To remove, by burning unwanted surface hairs or filaments, usually performed as a preliminary to bleaching and finishing.

34. **Sliver:** An assembly of fibers in continuous form without twist. The untangled fibers lie parallel and form a fine web of continuous strips or slivers.

35. SPINDLE: A long thin rod used for twisting and holding the spun thread when spinning.

36. SPINNING: Spinning is simply twisting wool strands. Coarser wool is spun into woolen yarn. Finer wool is spun into worsted yarn. The spinning process takes the woolen or worsted roving and twists it into yarn. Twisting wool strands increases the strength of the yarn and creates the continuous unbroken yarn necessary for weaving the cloth.

37. SPONGING: Steaming piece goods before made into garments.

38. STENTER TENTER: An open-width fabric-finishing machine in which the selvedges of a textile fabric are held by a pair of endless traveling chains to maintain weft tension.

39. STOCK DYED: Wool dyed immediately after it is washed and blended.

40. TRUCK (HAND TRUCK): Any of various low frames or platforms on wheels for carrying heavy articles as in a mill or warehouse.

41. TWIST: The number of times one inch of yarn is twisted.

42. WARP: In woven fabric, the yarns that run lengthwise and are interwoven with the filling (weft) yarns.

43. WEAVING: Produces fabric by interlacing lengthwise yarns (warp) with crosswise yarns (weft or filling).

44. WEFT: In woven fabric, the filling yarns that run perpendicular to the warp yarns.

45. WOOLEN YARN: Woolen fabrics are fuzzy, thick, and bulky and are made from shorter fibers one to three inches long which have been carded only.

46. WORSTED YARN: Worsted fabrics such as crepe and gabardine are made from wool three inches and longer that undergoes an extra process called step combing.